HEWLETT-WOODMERE PUBLIC LIBRARY
HEWLETT, NEW YORK

Leonard Bernstein
and American Music

Catherine Reef

Leonard Bernstein
and American Music

Catherine Reef

Greensboro, North Carolina

Modern Music Masters

Uh Huh!: The Story of Ray Charles

Reggae Poet: The Story of Bob Marley

Spin: The Story of Michael Jackson

Leonard Bernstein and American Music

For June Patterson, constant reader

Leonard Bernstein

Copyright © 2013 Morgan Reynolds Publishing

All rights reserved.
This book, or parts thereof, may not be reproduced in any form except by written consent of the publisher. For more information write: Morgan Reynolds Publishing, Inc., 620 South Elm Street, Suite 387, Greensboro, North Carolina 27406 USA

Library of Congress Cataloging-in-Publication Data

Reef, Catherine.
 Leonard Bernstein and American music / by Catherine Reef. -- 1st ed.
   p. cm. -- (Modern music masters)
 Includes bibliographical references.
 ISBN 978-1-59935-125-4 -- ISBN 978-1-59935-261-9 (e-book)
 1. Bernstein, Leonard, 1918-1990--Juvenile literature. 2. Musicians--United States--Biography--Juvenile literature. I. Title.
 ML3930.B48R44 2011
 780.92--dc22
 [B]
                            2010042593

Printed in the United States of America
First Edition

Contents

Chapter One	9	Music Was "It"
Chapter Two	19	The Wide World Beckons
Chapter Three	29	Seeking His Fortune
Chapter Four	39	Suddenly—Boom!
Chapter Five	49	Life, Love, and the World
Chapter Six	59	With His Whole Heart
Chapter Seven	69	A Double Man
Chapter Eight	79	Replying to Violence
Chapter Nine	91	Five Lives or So
Chapter Ten	101	Defiance
Timeline	108	
Sources	110	
Bibliography	118	
Web Sites	122	
The Major Works	123	
Index	125	

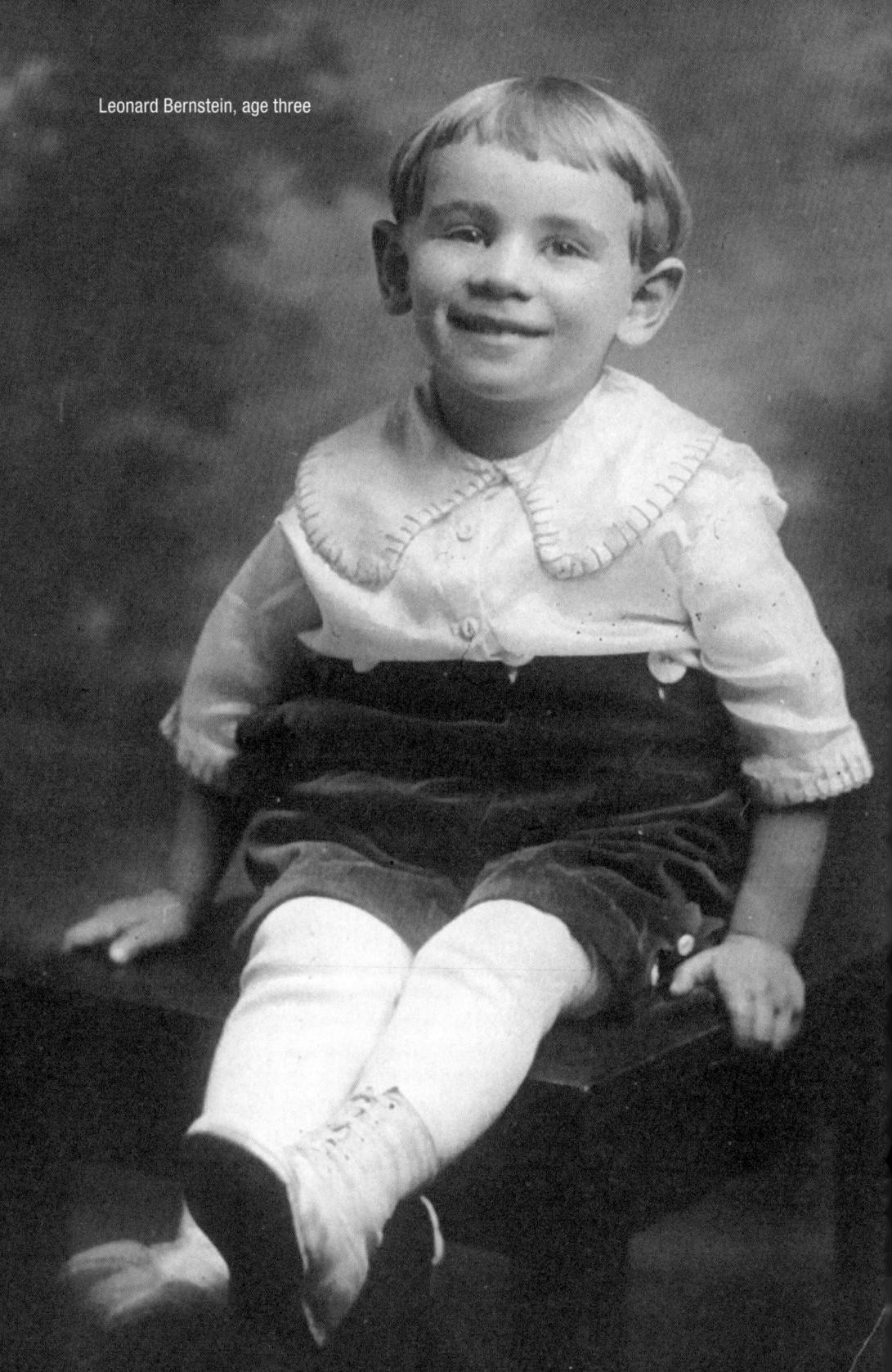
Leonard Bernstein, age three

Chapter One
Music Was "It"

Samuel Bernstein needed his rest, but how could he sleep with ten-year-old Lenny making so much racket? Day and night, the boy was pounding out songs he had learned from the radio. Hardworking Samuel regretted the day when the old upright piano came into the house, a gift from his sister Clara.

Lenny, meanwhile, was in heaven. "I remember touching this thing on the day it arrived, just stroking it and going mad," Leonard Bernstein said nearly sixty years later. "I knew, from that moment to this, that music was 'it.' There was no question in my mind that my life was to be about music."

His love of music would make him famous throughout the world. In the second half of the twentieth century, Leonard Bernstein would be celebrated as a conductor, pianist, and composer. Melodies and rhythms had sparked Lenny's interest before the piano came—even before he could walk or talk. His parents quickly learned to quiet their fussy baby by playing records on the Victrola. Lenny loved the popular song that went: "In the land of San Domingo/Lived a girl called Oh! By Jingo." As a toddler, he tapped out tunes with his fingers as he looked through the window of his Lawrence, Massachusetts, home. His mother, Jennie Bernstein, loved music, too, and always seemed to have a tune running through her head.

Samuel and Jennie's first child was born in Lawrence on August 25, 1918. They named him Louis, as Jennie's parents wished, but they called him a name they liked better, Leonard—or just Lenny. And they worried about his health. Born with a "delicate chest," Lenny was prone to colds and asthma. "Every time he had an attack, we thought he was going to die," Jennie Bernstein said. She stayed up many nights, boiling water to create the steam that would help Lenny breathe.

Lenny's parents were immigrants from Russia. They were among the 2 million Eastern European Jews who entered the United States in the late nineteenth and early twentieth centuries. Sam Bernstein had sailed alone to New York when he was sixteen years old. Determined to succeed, he spent three years studying English while he supported himself by cleaning fish. He traded the fish-cleaning job for a better one, and that job for one even better. He kept on moving up in this way, and by the time he met Jennie Resnick, he was making a good living selling beauty supplies to hairdressers in and around Boston.

Jennie had immigrated to the United States when she was seven years old. Her family had settled in Lawrence, an important center for the manufacture of cloth. Immigrants flocked to Lawrence from Europe and Canada to work in the town's factories, and they lived in neighborhoods with others from their homelands.

Jennie was a bright girl who did well in school and hoped to become a teacher. But the Resnicks were poor, so she gave up her dream. She was working in a factory that produced woolen cloth when she met Samuel Bernstein. Fun-loving Jennie liked the stories and jokes that Samuel told.

Samuel Bernstein was also a pious man, devoted to reading the Talmud, the sacred book of Jewish law. "His life's textbook is the Talmud. He finds an analogy in the Talmud for every problem that arises in his business," his son Leonard observed. On Friday evenings, Lenny sat beside his father in Temple Mishkan Tefila. He listened in wonder as the congregation's chief singer—the cantor—sang the ancient prayerful tunes of the Jewish Sabbath service. "And I used to weep just listening to the choir, cantor, and organ thundering out—it was a big influence on me," Bernstein recalled.

In 1922, when he was thirty years old, Samuel Bernstein started his own beauty-supply company, and it quickly prospered. As his

Chapter One: *Music Was "It"*

earnings rose, the Bernsteins traded houses the way Samuel once traded jobs. They moved again and again, always to a bigger house in a fancier suburb. In 1927, when they settled in Roxbury, Massachusetts, there were two children in the family. A girl, Shirley, had been born in 1923. A third child, Burton, would be born in 1932.

Lenny earned good grades at William Lloyd Garrison School, but he wanted to study more than history and spelling and penmanship. Once the piano came, he begged his parents for music lessons. The Bernsteins gave in and paid a neighborhood girl named Frieda Karp one dollar a week to instruct their son on the piano. She led Lenny through the beginning exercise books and taught him some of the simplest pieces by Frederic Chopin, Johann Sebastian Bach, and other great composers.

Then, after three years as Lenny's piano teacher, Frieda Karp gave up. "This boy is gifted," she told his parents. "I can't keep up with him." She told the Bernsteins to find a more advanced teacher at Boston's New England Conservatory of Music, one of the world's leading music schools.

Bernstein with his parents, Samuel and Jennie, and sister, Shirley, in 1935

They followed her advice, and Susan Williams, an instructor at the conservatory, agreed to be Leonard's teacher. But when Samuel Bernstein heard that she charged three dollars a week, he hit the ceiling. He refused to pay that much for piano lessons, although he could easily afford to do so. "He saw that things were getting serious," Leonard Bernstein said. "So the fights began."

"A *klezmer* you want to be?" Samuel Bernstein shouted at his son. Lenny's father had no idea that in the United States a musician could earn a good salary and the public's respect. He knew only about the *klezmer* musicians of Russia, men who wandered from one Jewish village to another. They earned a pittance playing at weddings and bar mitzvahs and had no permanent home. It seemed to him that Lenny was choosing this kind of life.

Lenny was determined to study with Williams, though, so he earned the money himself. "It was a big hardship but such fun because it made me independent of my father," Bernstein said. He formed a jazz band with two other boys, one who played the saxophone and another who played drums. On weekends, they entertained at weddings.

He also taught neighborhood children to play the piano, charging one dollar per lesson. His first student, a boy named Sid Ramin, became his friend for life. Lenny and Sid listened excitedly to a record of *Rhapsody in Blue,* a work for a piano and jazz band by American composer George Gershwin. Gershwin, like Lenny, was the son of Russian Jewish immigrants. In *Rhapsody in Blue,* he blended the styles of classical music and jazz. Lenny and Sid worked out their own arrangement of Gershwin's groundbreaking piece, trying to recreate the sound of a jazz band with their four hands on a piano keyboard.

Lenny was growing independent in other ways, as well. As a seventh grader, he commuted alone by train and streetcar to Boston Latin School. The oldest public school in the nation (dating back to 1635), Boston Latin accepted only the best students, and until 1972 it accepted only boys. Philip Marson, one of Lenny's favorite teachers, said that the school equipped students with "three indispensable qualifications: the ability to garner information; the possession of a storehouse of linguistic knowledge; and a desire to influence others." True to its name, Boston Latin School required students to complete six years of Latin, from grade seven through high school. Lenny also studied French, German, physics, history, and English. The teachers demanded hard work, but Leonard Bernstein loved the challenge. Marson recalled him sitting in the front of his English class, "lapping up everything I could dish out in drama and poetry."

After dismissal each afternoon, Lenny headed for Hebrew school to prepare for his bar mitzvah. In 1931, on the day he completed this sacred rite of passage, he stood in the synagogue before relatives and friends to declare that he had come of age in matters of faith. His father rewarded him with a baby grand piano.

Samuel Bernstein was of two minds about Lenny and his music. He worried about Lenny choosing a life of hardship and disappointment, but he also was proud of his son's talent. For this reason, he stood in the way of Lenny's musical ambitions at some times, yet gave him generous support at others. Samuel twice took his son to hear concerts in Boston's Symphony Hall, and he arranged for Lenny to perform for the Temple Brotherhood, a Jewish men's organization to which Samuel belonged. For this occasion, Lenny composed a piece of music inspired by a prayer his father sang in the shower.

When he had free time, Lenny played in neighborhood baseball games. He and his friend Eddie Ryack invented an imaginary country called Rybernia, with themselves as its leaders. They came up with the country's name by combining the first syllables of Ryack and Bernstein, and they pasted together its language, Rybernian, from snippets of the Yiddish and broken English they heard spoken by Jewish immigrants. Lenny taught this secret language to his sister and brother. He, Shirley, and Burton remembered how to speak Rybernian for the rest of their lives.

13

Young Lenny played piano duets at parties with his friend Mildred Spiegel. Mildred, a dedicated music student two years older than Lenny, urged him to find a better teacher than Susan Williams. She convinced him to audition for Heinrich Gebhard, a renowned piano instructor who lived in Boston. Gebhard listened to Lenny play and encouraged him to stick with the piano, but he declined to take the boy on as a student. Instead, he referred Lenny to another fine teacher, Helen Coates, who had devoted her life to piano education. Stiff and proper most of the time, Coates responded with excitement to Lenny's talent. She offered to teach him, but there was just one problem: she charged six dollars an hour for lessons.

The high fee caused Samuel Bernstein to catch his breath, but this time he agreed to pay. He confessed to Helen Coates that he had given up any hope of Leonard following him into business. "I do realize that there are even greater achievements to be made in the musical field," he said, "and I trust that Leonard will eventually become one of the talented pianists." Samuel sponsored a series of live broadcasts featuring Leonard at the piano on WBZ, a Boston radio station. Still, Lenny had not heard the last of his father's objections to a musical career.

The boy from Roxbury was one of the finest students Coates had ever taught. He was such an eager pupil that the hour-long lessons Samuel paid for always seemed too brief. Lenny often stayed on in Coates's studio for another hour or two to perfect the fine points of piano technique. Between lessons, he practiced on the piano at home, loudly and long. When neighbors complained about the noise, Jennie Bernstein assured them that one day they would pay to hear her son play in a concert hall.

In 1932, the Bernsteins built a summer home in the vacation community of Sharon, Massachusetts. While their father commuted to his office in Boston, twenty miles away, the children swam in Lake Massapoag. Lenny breathed clean, fresh air that was thought to aid his asthma, and he grew stronger. One summer, Samuel put him to work in his company's shipping room and paid him one dollar a day, but Lenny hated the job and quit after just two weeks.

He was happier directing shows that featured Shirley and his friends from neighboring cottages. In 1934, the "Sharon Players" staged a shortened, comic version of *Carmen*, Georges Bizet's tragic

Chapter One: *Music Was "It"*

opera about a beautiful Spanish gypsy. Girls in men's trousers sang the male roles, and boys wearing dresses sang the female parts. Lenny, disguised in a bright red wig, sang the role of Carmen. He and his friends filled the performance with jokes about their friends and neighbors in Sharon, many of whom were in the audience.

Carmen was such a big hit that in following years the players staged two comic operettas written by the British team of W. S. Gilbert and Arthur Sullivan: *The Mikado*, set in Japan, and *H.M.S. Pinafore,* a satire set aboard a British naval ship. The players held most of their rehearsals in the Bernsteins' cottage. "Strewn around our living room were thirty-odd young performers, draped carelessly over the furniture and sprawled on the floor, singing away at the top of their voices to Lenny's direction," Shirley Bernstein recalled.

The singing caused no problem on weekdays, when Samuel Bernstein was at work, but it bothered him on weekends. "He couldn't read the Talmud," Jennie Bernstein explained. "There was too much noise and excitement. The doors were slamming, in and out, in and out. Sam liked quiet, relaxing."

An 1896 poster of Georges Bizet's *Carmen*, starring Rosabel Morrison

At the end of summer in 1933, the Bernsteins moved into a new brick house in fashionable Newton, Massachusetts. They lived a comfortable life at a time when millions of Americans were losing their jobs, their savings, and their homes. In 1929, the United States had entered the Great Depression, a period of financial hardship that was more severe and longer lasting than any that had come before. Thousands of men wandered Boston's streets, looking for work.

15

On New Year's Day, 1931, unemployed men lined up for blocks along Hanover Street to receive a free holiday meal. The following Christmas, volunteers handed out 1,600 pairs of shoes to some of the city's desperate children. The shoes helped the children stay warm, and they enabled many to attend school. "Underwear can be made from sugar sacks. Clothes can be patched and remade," wrote two journalists who reported on education in the 1930s. "Shoes seem the insurmountable obstacle to school attendance in many impoverished families."

Hairdressers catered to those women who still had money to spend, so Samuel Bernstein's beauty-supply company weathered the depression. The Bernsteins could afford to own a car, and at sixteen, Lenny obtained his driver's license. At this time, he also changed his name legally from Louis to Leonard. A handsome boy with wavy, dark hair and intense, hazel eyes, Leonard was nearing his adult height of five feet, eight inches. He had taken up smoking—an addiction he never would be able to break.

Lenny often ventured into Boston, alone or with Mildred Spiegel. One night, the two heard the Boston Symphony Orchestra (BSO) in

Dr. Serge Koussevitzky conducting the Boston Symphony Orchestra during a practice session in Symphony Hall, Boston

concert, conducted by Serge Koussevitzky, the orchestra's Russian-born music director. Koussevitzky's vast knowledge of music and superior conducting skills had earned Boston a worldwide reputation for fine orchestral music.

When the performance ended and the rest of the audience rose to applaud, Lenny stayed in his seat. Mildred thought he had disliked the performance, but Lenny insisted that he loved it. He envied Koussevitzky, for whom the orchestra was a finely tuned instrument. Under the baton of this great conductor, the musicians brought forth all the beauty, gaiety, passion, and anguish the composers had written into their music.

Lenny explored his musical goals in an essay written during his senior year for Philip Marson's English class. "There is never a time when I do not prefer playing my piano to any other sort of work or recreation," he wrote. "It is inexplicably true that because of rather than in spite of home discouragement, I am filled all the more with the desire for a musical life."

At school, he performed piano solos, accompanied by the student orchestra. He sang in the glee club, and he helped compose his class song, "All for One and One for All." Like every senior at Boston Latin School, Lenny read thick books on philosophy, history, and the arts. He excelled in the classes that interested him, but he put less effort into the ones that bored him. As a result, he graduated in 1935 at the top of his class in English but with a poor grade in history.

More than ever, music was "it" for Leonard Bernstein. He was ready to devote his life to music, but how? Becoming a concert pianist demanded many hours of practice, but Lenny had too much energy to sit still for so long. And he had too much curiosity to limit himself to performing at the keyboard. He wanted to know everything about music: how it was written and understood, how it had changed over the centuries, and how it moved the human spirit. He wanted, too, to immerse himself in the world of ideas. He chose to continue his studies at Harvard University, in nearby Cambridge, Massachusetts. Harvard was the oldest college in the United States, and the most revered.

Bernstein in 1939

Chapter Two
The Wide World Beckons

In 1935, Leonard Bernstein was among the 750 freshmen who came to Harvard from all over the United States and from countries throughout the world. The new students moved into residence halls and settled down to college life.

Leonard registered for classes in English literature, Italian, German, fine art, and general music. He soon discovered that the students at Harvard learned about music the same way they mastered history or economics. They read books, wrote papers, and listened to lectures. They barely heard a note, and never played one. Music "was meant to be seen and not heard," joked a Harvard graduate.

Outside class, the students joined the many clubs and activities that Harvard offered. One Harvard professor observed: "Editors of a college paper, debaters in a college team, students working side by side in a laboratory—or even in athletics—are laying the foundation of permanent friendship." The clubs and teams were open to students unequally, however. Jews, who comprised about 15 percent of the student body in 1935, were barred from joining most fraternities. Leonard Bernstein also could not join the Signet Society, a club for students interested in the arts, because he was a Jew. He never performed in plays staged by the Hasty Pudding theatrical club for the same reason.

Leonard responded by forming his own music club, which met in the attic of a professor's home. The club members drank tea and listened to music that was daring and new, such as *The Rite of Spring,* by Russian composer Igor Stravinsky. Even the most cultured listeners had protested the harsh rhythms and clashing notes of Stravinsky's ballet when it was first performed in 1913. Many had detested its content as well. *The Rite of Spring,* which depicts a pagan fertility ritual, ends with the spectacle of human sacrifice. "Music has never been the same since that performance," Bernstein said. "Stravinsky created a revolution."

Maybe so, but *The Rite of Spring* was composed during a time of great experimentation in all the arts. Pablo Picasso and other cubist painters were breaking time-honored rules of composition. Writers were employing the stream-of-consciousness style, recording the random thoughts that passed through their characters' minds. Art had entered the modern age, and the public was left to make sense of much that was strange and controversial.

Lenny was a popular performer when students gathered informally around a piano to sing. He also played at events held to raise funds for political causes, such as the civil war in Spain. Many Americans supported the loyal Spaniards who were fighting General Francisco Franco's attempt to seize control of their government. Franco's forces were getting help from Nazi Germany and its totalitarian ally, Fascist Italy.

Igor Stravinsky applauds at the close of a performance of *The Rite of Spring* by the Boston Symphony Orchestra at the Theatre des Champs Elysees, in Paris, France, on May 8, 1952.

Chapter Two: *The Wide World Beckons*

On October 31, 1937, Lenny played in public with the State Symphony Orchestra. This was one of many musical ensembles formed by the Works Progress Administration (WPA), a government agency that gave jobs to unemployed Americans during the Great Depression. At this concert, Bernstein played with "assurance and a considerable technique to clothe his genuine talent," observed the music critic for the *Boston Herald,* who was in the audience.

Leonard continued taking piano lessons while at Harvard, but now he studied with Heinrich Gebhard, the teacher who had turned him down when he was fourteen. He thrived under Gebhard's patient nurturing. "Anything that I did that pleased him was magnified into a miracle by his enthusiasms; my failures were minimized and lovingly corrected," Bernstein said. "And all was bathed in the glow of wonder, of constant astonishment."

Gebhard also coached Leonard in composition, because this eager student was writing music of his own. In January 1937, Leonard played a piece that he had written for the famed Greek conductor Dimitri Mitropoulos, who visited Harvard while in town to conduct the Boston Symphony Orchestra. Mitropoulos was so impressed with Bernstein's ability that he invited the young man to attend his rehearsals with the BSO. This was a chance not to be missed. So even though exams were coming up, Lenny spent a week at Symphony Hall, watching Mitropoulos and the orchestra practice. He learned what a conductor does by observing Mitropoulos at work. He saw how a conductor studies a score, or the written music, which shows the notes that the various instruments play.

Once he had stored every detail in his memory, Mitropoulos decided how to interpret the work. He thought about how the musicians could best communicate ideas and feelings the composer hoped to evoke. Should they pause a little longer before rushing into a thrilling cascade of notes? Should the horns quiet down to let the strings be heard? This was the true art of conducting, because notes and markings on paper cannot convey such profound thoughts and emotions. The conductor then taught the orchestra to play the music as he understood it, and when the hundred musicians could perform the piece together as one, they were ready for an audience.

Sober-minded Boston had never seen such an active conductor. Lean and tall with alert blue eyes, Mitropoulos leaped onto the stage like an athlete. He used his whole body to conduct, jumping into the air, crouching like a predator, and shaking his fist like an angry demon. Unlike most conductors, he used no baton, preferring to lead the orchestra with empty hands. The musicians—and the audience—responded with excitement, and Leonard Bernstein absorbed it all. Mitropoulos advised the young man to work hard at his music and never to lose sight of his goals.

That summer, Lenny took a job as music counselor at Camp Onota, a sleep-away camp for children near Pittsfield, Massachusetts. He led the campers in song, helped them put on plays and concerts, and joined them for baseball games. "Lenny impressed us greatly with his piano playing," remembered one camper, but "on the baseball field he was hitless and never could advance the runner from first to second."

It was lucky for Lenny that the summer's big event took place on stage, and not on the baseball diamond. He directed the campers in *The Pirates of Penzance,* Gilbert and Sullivan's comic operetta about a band of softhearted pirates. The youth who starred as the Pirate King, Adolph Green of New York City, knew almost as much about music as Bernstein did. He had never taken lessons but had taught himself by listening to records and remembering everything he heard. He could sing symphonies from beginning to end, mimicking the sounds of the instruments. Green and Bernstein quickly became friends. They hiked in the hills around Camp Onota, conversing about music and books. Green believed that he had befriended a genius, and that his life was forever changed. "I felt the fresh air of 1,000,000 windows opening simultaneously," he commented.

Lenny brought his new friend to visit the Bernstein cottage in Sharon. While the two young men quizzed each other about music, and Adolph Green sang and made funny noises, Samuel Bernstein nervously paced. "Who is that nut?" he asked his wife. "I want him out of my house!"

There were serious moments that summer, as well. On July 11, Lenny learned from the radio that George Gershwin, the composer of *Rhapsody in Blue* and other great works, had died of a brain tumor at age thirty-eight. It was parents' visiting day at Camp Onota, and at lunch the dining hall was noisy with chatter. Lenny walked to the piano at the front of the room and played a loud chord.

When the voices fell silent, he announced that America's greatest Jewish composer was dead. He sat down and played *Prelude Number 2,* one of Gershwin's best-known piano pieces, requesting no applause.

At summer's end, Leonard Bernstein returned to Harvard and to piano study. With Heinrich Gebhard's help, he mastered the *Piano Variations,* a recent work by America's foremost living composer, Aaron Copland. Copland began the *Piano Variations* with a perplexing series of notes and jarring chords that few people in the 1930s would have called music.

American composer Aaron Copland leans on his piano at his home in Ossining, New York, on June 28, 1956.

Bernstein loved the hard, drum-like sound of Copland's *Piano Variations*. "A new world of music had opened to me in this work," one that was "extreme, prophetic, clangorous, fiercely dissonant, intoxicating," he claimed. He liked to play the *Piano Variations* at parties, and he joked that this was a great way to empty a room.

Later that fall, he and a Harvard friend named I. B. Cohen went to New York City to see a program of modern dance. They were the guests of Cohen's friend Muriel Rukeyser, a poet. During the intermission, Rukeyser introduced the two students to the person sitting on Lenny's right, "an odd-looking man in his thirties," as Bernstein recalled, who had "a pair of glasses resting on his great hooked nose and a mouth filled with teeth flashing a wide grin." This gentleman, Rukeyser said, was Aaron Copland. "I almost fell out of the balcony," Bernstein admitted.

It happened to be Copland's birthday, so he invited his new friends to a party at his apartment after the show. There, Lenny entertained the guests by playing the *Piano Variations* from memory, and this time no one left the room. Copland was generous with his time and willing to help beginning composers. He looked over Bernstein's compositions and advised him to keep only the best. He showed Bernstein how to edit his own work, how to cut out passages that added nothing or were out of keeping with the rest of a piece. "He taught me a tremendous amount about taste, style, and consistency in music," Bernstein said.

Bernstein turned to Copland, who was eighteen years older, when he needed advice. He wrote to the composer in March 1938, after the armed forces of Nazi Germany occupied Austria. The Nazis were in the beginning stages of a campaign to dominate Europe and suppress Jews and others not of "Aryan," or pure German, heritage. Bernstein questioned the wisdom of devoting his life to art when human progress seemed to be coming undone. "With every element that we thought had refined human living and made what we called civilization being actively forgotten," he asked, "what chance is there?"

Copland counseled his young friend to be optimistic and consider the whole of human history, including those events that had happened in the distant past and those yet to occur. "Man has a long time to go. Art is quite young," he wrote. Then he added: "Aren't you always curious to see what tomorrow will bring?"

Lenny and his college friends stayed up late at night discussing the troubling news from Europe. Lenny dragged himself to morning classes after these long bull sessions, and his studies suffered. He earned some As, but most of his grades were Bs and Cs.

Yet he threw his energy into projects that captured his interest, such as writing his senior thesis. For this final paper, titled "The Absorption of Race Elements in American Music," he showed how the music of America's diverse ethnic and racial groups had influenced Gershwin, Copland, and other American composers. The blues and jazz of African Americans, the rhythms of Latin America, the hymns of old New England, the sacred Jewish music of his childhood—all these streams had flowed together to "become the mighty American river which is now, for the first time, pouring its fullness . . . into the sea of world music."

He also put together a student production of *The Cradle Will Rock*, by the composer Marc Blitzstein. This musical show concerns an effort to bring steelworkers into a labor union. A year earlier, *The Cradle Will Rock* was set to be performed on Broadway, in New York City. But on opening night, government censors locked the theater. They objected to the content of Blitzstein's musical, because in the 1930s many union organizers belonged to the Communist Party. Blitzstein promptly rented another theater nearby. There, cast members sang their songs from the audience while he accompanied them on piano. Because the cast performed without scenery or props, Blitzstein called out the scene changes from the piano. The evening is remembered as a milestone in the history of free speech in the United States.

Not only did Lenny direct this show at Harvard, but he also was onstage throughout the performance, playing the piano and announcing the scene changes, as Blitzstein had done. He played two small roles, as well. He gave a part to his sister, Shirley, who drove to Harvard every evening after dinner to rehearse, although at fifteen she was too young to have a driver's license. Lenny's energy was contagious. The students had only ten days to learn their parts, but he was sure the show would be a smash. He was so confident that he invited Marc Blitzstein to attend. And to his surprise, the composer came.

Blitzstein flew to Boston in time to see the morning dress rehearsal and talk about music with Bernstein during an afternoon walk along the Charles River. He saw the opening performance and played the

Chapter Two: *The Wide World Beckons*

piano at the cast party afterward. Back home in New York, he wrote to Bernstein: "It all packed a thrilling wallop for me—second only to the original NY opening."

Despite his careless approach to study, Leonard Bernstein graduated from Harvard with honors in music. Still holding a small hope that Lenny would follow him into business, his father offered him a job at one hundred dollars a week. But a wider world of music had opened to Lenny during his college years. He had met two successful composers, Aaron Copland and Marc Blitzstein, and a famous conductor, Dimitri Mitropoulos. He knew that, somewhere beyond Boston, this world held a place for him. In early July, he took off for New York City to share an apartment with his friend from Camp Onota, Adolph Green.

American composer Marc Blitzstein during a BBC broadcast in London, on August 4, 1943

Clockwise from left: Bernstein and performers Jerome Robbins, Betty Comden, and Adolph Green

Chapter Three

Seeking His Fortune

New Yorkers wanting to see fresh, new talent flocked to the nightspots of Greenwich Village, the neighborhood that was home to artists, writers, and bohemians. One of the hottest acts to catch in the summer of 1939 was the Revuers, a troupe of young performers who sang, danced, and clowned on stage. One of the Revuers was Adolph Green.

The Revuers performed at the Village Vanguard, a narrow basement with a homemade curtain hanging at one end to make a stage. They wrote their own skits and songs, and they each earned five dollars a night.

After attending his friend's show only once, Bernstein could play all the tunes from memory. Late that first night, after all the customers had gone, he entertained at the piano for hours, switching easily from the pounding rhythms of boogie-woogie to the intricate web work of Johann Sebastian Bach. Betty Comden, Green's fellow Revuer, had never met anyone like sparkling, high-spirited Bernstein. She went home and woke up her mother to say, "I met a real genius."

That summer, Bernstein spent many nights at the Village Vanguard or at Lewisohn Stadium, where he listened to outdoor concerts of classical music. During the day, he composed music of his own. He began a piece for a singer and orchestra based on the Lamentations of Jeremiah, biblical verses said to have been written by the prophet Jeremiah. Jews read them on Tisha B'Av, the day when they mourn the destruction of the temple in ancient Jerusalem by the Babylonians. Bernstein called his piece "Hebrew Song."

Paying work as a musician in New York was out of his reach without a union card. He could join the musicians' union once he had lived in the city for six months, but Adolph Green had the apartment only through August, and a place of his own cost more than Bernstein could afford. At summer's end, he had four dollars to his name. He joined his family in Sharon, where he thought about what to do with all his talent, education, and ambition.

Three weeks later, he was back in New York, summoned by the conductor Dimitri Mitropoulos. Mitropoulos had been thinking about Bernstein's future, too, and asked if he wanted to study conducting. Bernstein had broad knowledge and great musical

The main building of the Curtis Institute of Music in Philadelphia, Pennsylvania

Chapter Three: *Seeking His Fortune*

ability—just the qualities a good conductor needed. Bernstein had thought about conducting once in a while, but never seriously. Yet at this moment, it sounded like a brilliant idea. He decided that conducting was all he wanted to do.

It was too late to apply to the Juilliard School, the prestigious conservatory in New York City; the fall class was already full. But there was an opening at the Curtis School of Music in Philadelphia, and Aaron Copland knew Fritz Reiner, the head of conducting studies at Curtis. Copland was more than happy to write a letter recommending his young friend. Before the school would accept him, though, Bernstein had to pass a tough exam, demonstrating his knowledge of musical works.

He spent the weekend before the test studying at Copland's summer home in Woodstock, New York. Copland's cats and the pollen that filled the country air triggered Bernstein's allergies, and he showed up at Curtis on the day of his exam with swollen eyes and a running nose. Still, he managed to pass.

His next challenge was to figure out how to afford living in Philadelphia. A scholarship covered his tuition, but he needed money for rent and food, and his parents refused to help. Samuel Bernstein announced that paying for four years at Harvard was enough. He had two more children to educate, and he claimed that Bernstein was wasting his time. The important conductors came from Europe, never from America.

In 1939, this was true. Mitropoulos was Greek, Koussevitzky was Russian, and Reiner was Hungarian. Artur Rodzinski, who directed the New York Philharmonic Orchestra, was from Poland, and Bruno Walter, another of the world's great conductors, had been born in Germany. Yet Mitropoulos believed that an American could achieve success—even greatness—as a conductor, so he gave Bernstein $75 a month to cover his expenses. Bernstein rented a cheap room with a view of trashcans and buckled down to work.

The Curtis Institute of Music was still new, having opened in 1924, but it was housed in an old building with high ceilings and thick carpets. It was a small school, where teachers worked closely with their students and expected excellence. At Curtis, Bernstein learned conducting from Reiner, a teacher who demanded hours of study. Reiner insisted that his conducting students know what every musician in the orchestra was playing at every moment. He kept his body still and used a long baton to communicate with the orchestra.

Bernstein studied the piano with Russian-born teacher Isabelle Vengerova, who "scared the daylights out of me," he said. After feeling the force of her mighty temper, no student dared to disagree with her or show up for a lesson unprepared. Vengerova taught Bernstein to listen to himself while he played the piano as carefully as a conductor listened to an orchestra. As he overcame his trembling fear of her, she taught him to relax at the keyboard and draw beautiful sounds from the piano.

Bernstein was older than his fellow students and often more knowledgeable. "He was almost like a teacher to me," said Lukas Foss, who was a teenager when he studied alongside Bernstein at the Curtis Institute.

"I work and work and work," Bernstein wrote to Helen Coates, "and do nothing else, except sleep plenty." He worked hard through the fall and cold Philadelphia winter. As spring lengthened and warmed the days, he heard some exciting news. A summer music school was about to open at Tanglewood, a country estate near the Berkshire Mountains of Massachusetts. Tanglewood was the summer home of the Boston Symphony Orchestra. Music lovers flocked there to hear concerts under the stars.

Conductor Serge Koussevitzky hoped to draw young musicians to the site, to "bring them into association with the leading artists and scholars of the day," he stated. "'Tanglewood' will be a place for those who wish to refresh the mind and personality by the experience of the best in music and the related arts." Koussevitzky was going to teach a select group of conducting students, and he boldly predicted that Tanglewood would produce five conductors of genius within five years.

Bernstein asked Aaron Copland to speak to Koussevitzky and recommend him. Then, too impatient to wait for his friend to act, he rushed to Boston and went backstage at Symphony Hall, where he introduced himself to the conductor. Koussevitzky chatted with

Bernstein for several minutes and welcomed him into the class at Tanglewood.

Koussevitzky believed that it was more important for Americans to practice the arts in 1940 than ever before. Not only had war disrupted artistic progress in Europe, but also fascist and totalitarian governments were suppressing artists' freedom to create. "If ever there was a time to speak of music, it is now in the New World," he told the students at Tanglewood.

Koussevitzky showed Leonard Bernstein a whole different style of conducting. He led the orchestra with his entire body, swaying, sweeping his arms, and changing the expression on his face. He told the students to avoid standing stiffly like Fritz Reiner, and he brought

Boston Symphony conductor Serge Koussevitzky (left) goes over a score with Leonard Bernstein in Boston, Massachusetts, on February 14, 1944.

in a dance instructor to show them how to move. He ordered them to practice conducting in front of a mirror. "I did this one day by myself and fell about in such laughter that I couldn't repeat it," Bernstein said. Yet he was finding his own conducting style, one that blended Reiner's attention to detail with Koussevitzky's flow of feeling. Like Dimitri Mitropoulos, Bernstein conducted without a baton.

The students at Tanglewood worked like mad from morning until night. Bernstein was absorbing so much knowledge that he felt like a sponge. Koussevitzky soon called him by an affectionate nickname, "Lenyushka," and predicted that he would become a great conductor. Koussevitzky warned Lenyushka that because of anti-Semitism, a conductor with the name Leonard Bernstein might never be invited to perform in great concert houses like New York's Carnegie Hall. He urged the young man to change his name to the Scottish-sounding Leonard Burns. This was something that Bernstein refused to do. "I will have to make it with the name Leonard Bernstein or not at all," he said.

The students each had a chance to conduct the Institute Orchestra, which consisted of young people studying instruments. When it was Bernstein's turn, his family drove to Tanglewood to see him perform. Shirley was about to enter college, and Burton was eight. Bernstein conducted a modern piece, the Second Symphony by Randall Thompson, an American composer.

Before the summer classes ended, Bernstein led professional musicians for the first time when he led the Boston Pops Orchestra. He also strengthened his friendship with Aaron Copland, who taught composition at Tanglewood. He returned to Philadelphia already looking forward to another summer of music in the Berkshires.

That fall, Bernstein played piano duets with his girlfriend, sixteen-year-old Shirley Gabis, who lived in an apartment near the Curtis Institute. "There was so much banging away on the piano that finally the chandelier broke in the apartment below and my mother got an eviction notice," Gabis remembered. Bernstein was spending much of his free time with Shirley, but he also felt drawn to an artist, who was a young man. He was starting to feel attracted to both women and men.

The school year ended in spring with a flurry of performances. On April 26, 1941, Bernstein conducted the Curtis Institute Orchestra in a radio concert, and on May 3, with Aaron Copland watching, he received his diploma in conducting. He had earned straight As in everything but piano. Vengerova had given him an A+.

Bernstein said goodbye to Shirley Gabis and spent the summer of 1941 at Tanglewood, learning more about conducting. Then he waited to hear from an orchestra that wanted to hire an American conductor.

He waited through the fall, living in an apartment in Boston, where his father paid the rent.

Meanwhile, Bernstein decided to give piano lessons. He had earned money teaching his friends as a boy, and now that he was grown and had studied for many years, he could charge a higher fee. He sent out cards announcing that Leonard Bernstein was opening a studio for the teaching of piano, but they brought in only one student. This was because Bernstein's timing could not have been worse. He mailed his announcements on December 5, 1941. Two days later, the armed forces of Japan attacked the U.S. naval base at Pearl Harbor, Hawaii, drawing the United States into the Second World War. Piano lessons were the last thing on most people's minds.

All around him, young men enlisted in the military to fight the Japanese in the South Pacific and the Germans and other Axis Powers in Europe and North Africa. Bernstein felt ashamed to be out of uniform, but the army had rejected him because of his asthma. Music helped people forget the fears and worries caused by war, so he felt useful playing the piano in Boston concerts.

After another summer at Tanglewood, he went to New York City, this time "to seek my fortune," he said, as a conductor. He moved into a cheap basement room and conducted here and there while hunting for steady work. He attracted some attention; one critic called his conducting "superb and musicianly." Still, no permanent job offers came his way, and Bernstein grew discouraged. Aaron Copland counseled him to be patient, saying, "Don't expect miracles." Breaking into the New York music world took time.

Bernstein did some composing to fill his empty days. He wrote a playful set of songs titled *I Hate Music!* He called them "kid songs," because their words reflect the thoughts of curious children. A little girl named Barbara wonders where babies come from; a child imagines living in a world with nine moons. "I hate music! But I like to sing," insists the child in the third song, who says that "music" belongs in stuffy concert halls. In the fourth song, a child tells a riddle, and in the fifth, a girl begs to be taken seriously. When she tells adults what is on her mind, they merely say, "Isn't she sweet? She wants to know everything!" The girl asks her audience, "Don't you?"

Bernstein also expanded his "Hebrew Song," making it part of a longer work, the *Jeremiah* Symphony. He divided this symphony into three sections, or movements, that follow the story of Jeremiah. In the first movement, titled "Prophecy," the horns introduce a simple melody that brings to mind the voice of Jeremiah delivering a message from God. Jeremiah warns the people of Jerusalem that their city will be destroyed unless they abandon their unholy ways. Heavy drumbeats punctuate the phrases and stress their solemn importance.

Yet as the livelier second movement, "Profanation," makes plain, the people ignore the prophet and pursue their ungodly lives. The music suggests a playful dance and the bustle of commerce. Only the movement's turbulent end makes plain that the prophecy has been fulfilled. The city has been destroyed.

In the third movement, "Lamentation," Bernstein draws directly from the Book of Lamentations. A soprano sings in Hebrew of the friendless, weeping city. She speaks to God, asking: "Wherefore dost Thou forget us forever, / And forsake us so long a time?"

The events described in the Book of Lamentations took place more than five hundred years before the start of the Christian era. Still, the despair conveyed by Bernstein's symphony had meaning in 1943, when many thousands of European Jews were dying in Nazi concentration camps and felt that they, too, had been forsaken. "How can I be blind to the problems of my own people?" Bernstein asked. "I'd give everything I have to be able to strike a death blow at fascism."

Bernstein had plenty of reason to hope, though. On his twenty-fifth birthday, August 25, 1943, he received the best present a beginning conductor could hope for: an invitation from Artur Rodzinski, the director of the New York Philharmonic Orchestra, to be his assistant. As Rodzinski's understudy, Bernstein would attend all the rehearsals, learn all the music that the orchestra was performing, and be ready to step in on short notice if Rodzinski or a guest conductor fell ill. Many years had passed since an assistant director had filled in, but the assistant needed to be prepared. As his reward for being always ready, in spring he would conduct the New York Philharmonic in its home, the city's famed Carnegie Hall.

Bernstein moved into a lonely, colorless room above Carnegie Hall. He spent many solitary hours there, memorizing the orchestra's music. He ate breakfast at the counter of a nearby drugstore, beside anonymous New Yorkers.

Chapter Three: *Seeking His Fortune*

The concert season began in the fall, when New Yorkers were home from their summer vacations. After the first hectic month of performances, Artur Rodzinski took a break. The famous Bruno Walter was to conduct the New York Philharmonic for two weeks while Rodzinski relaxed at his country home in Massachusetts.

Rodzinski was away on November 13 when opera star Jennie Tourel sang Bernstein's *I Hate Music!* at New York's Town Hall, a popular place for concerts. The Russian-born Tourel had recently moved to the United States, and American music lovers were eager to hear her perform. Bernstein's mother, father, and eleven-year-old brother took a train to New York to attend the big event.

The audience loved Tourel and everything she sang, and they went wild for *I Hate Music!* It was a short piece, but "people yelled and stamped and cheered and I had to take a bow," Bernstein reported. He celebrated at a party after the show and came home to his Carnegie Hall room as the sun was about to rise.

The jangling telephone woke him at 9 a.m. The caller told a groggy Bernstein that Bruno Walter was sick with the flu. The Philharmonic was counting on him to lead the orchestra that afternoon. This would be no ordinary concert, because it was to be broadcast over the radio. Bernstein would be conducting not only for the audience at Carnegie Hall, but also for listeners throughout the United States.

Leonard Bernstein in 1940

Chapter Four
Suddenly — Boom!

Leonard Bernstein had six hours to prepare for the most important afternoon of his young career. He went to Bruno Walter's hotel and listened as the ailing conductor, wrapped in a blanket, pointed out the tricky spots in the day's musical scores. At the corner drugstore, the pharmacist gave him two pills and instructions to swallow them before going onstage. The first pill supposedly would calm his nerves, and the second was meant to boost his energy. The other Bernsteins canceled their plans to return to Boston—this concert was too important to miss.

The hours flew by. At three o'clock, people across the country turned on their radios to hear the New York Philharmonic Orchestra, conducted by the great Bruno Walter. The audience in Carnegie Hall chatted, ignoring the squeaks and groans that came from the musicians tuning their instruments. The hall fell silent only when a balding man with a long face walked to center stage. He was Bruno Zirato, the orchestra's business manager. Speaking with an Italian accent, he announced that Bruno Walter was ill and would not be conducting that day. Instead, the nation would welcome a new American conductor: Leonard Bernstein.

It was a historic moment. Never before had a conductor born and trained in the United States led a major orchestra. Bernstein understood

Bernstein conducting the New York City Symphony in 1945

Chapter Four: *Suddenly—Boom!*

that a great deal depended on him. His success that afternoon would open doors for other young Americans, just as his failure would shut those doors for many years to come. As the disappointed audience tamely clapped, Bernstein took the pills from his pocket and tossed them across the floor. He told himself, "I'm going to do this on my own."

Bernstein hopped onto the podium, wearing his one good suit, as countless details ran through his mind. The first piece on the program, the *Manfred Overture,* by composer Robert Schumann, was also the trickiest, because it began with three fast chords, played one right after another. The first chord was the toughest of all, because unless all the musicians started playing at the very same instant, the result would be a noisy mess. In Carnegie Hall and across the country, people held their breath. Bernstein raised his arms, gave the signal to start, and he and the orchestra nailed it.

From that moment on, the music soared. The audience applauded with gusto for the *Manfred Overture.* They clapped so much for the second piece, a modern work, that Bernstein took four bows. Everyone listening understood that this was the launch of a great career. When the concert ended, the audience went wild. "The house roared like one giant animal in a zoo," Leonard's brother, Burton, recalled. Bernstein had "prodigious talent," boasted Artur Rodzinski, who had driven to New York from Massachusetts and reached Carnegie Hall in time for the intermission. A telegram arrived from Serge Koussevitzky in Boston: "LISTENING NOW; WONDERFUL."

One glowing face stood out in the crowd of well-wishers. It belonged to Samuel Bernstein. His father was "dazzled, bewildered, stupefied," Leonard said. "And he suddenly realized that it was all possible." Bernstein decided, then and there, to dedicate the *Jeremiah* Symphony to his father. In the weeks that followed, Samuel Bernstein defended his past efforts to discourage Bernstein from pursuing music. "I'm very proud of Lenny," he said, "but the Talmud teaches us, 'Don't expect miracles.'"

The public welcomed good news in wartime, so the *New York Times* printed the story of Bernstein's triumph on its front page. Suddenly, Leonard Bernstein was a star. Reporters called to interview him, actors and athletes asked to meet him, and music lovers sent him fan letters. Invitations to conduct poured in from orchestras in other cities.

41

On January 28, 1944, Bernstein led the Pittsburgh Symphony Orchestra in the world's first performance of his own composition, the *Jeremiah* Symphony. The audience loved Bernstein's symphony, and the New York Music Critics Circle voted it the best new classical work of the season. Over the next three years, Bernstein would conduct the *Jeremiah* Symphony throughout the United States and in several foreign countries.

All kinds of opportunities came his way. One fall night in 1943, he answered a knock at his door to find a young man his own age standing on the other side. He was Jerome Robbins, an up-and-coming dancer with the Ballet Theatre. A son of Jewish immigrants, like Bernstein, Robbins had grown up in Weehawken, New Jersey, where his father manufactured women's underwear.

Robbins had an idea for a new ballet called *Fancy Free,* about three sailors on shore leave in New York City, with twenty-four hours to see the sights and meet girls. The ballet was to reflect wartime New York and include the jumping, swinging popular dances of the day, like the Lindy Hop. Overshadowing the sailors' happiness would be the knowledge that when shore leave ended, they were shipping off to war. Robbins planned to choreograph the new ballet (design its dances), and he invited Bernstein to compose the music for it.

Bernstein hummed a tune he had jotted down that afternoon, and Robbins shouted: "That's it, that's what I had in mind!" The little melody had the distinct American sound that Robbins sought. "We went crazy," Bernstein said. "I began developing the theme right there in his presence. Thus the ballet was born."

They worked together on the music and choreography when they were both in town, and they worked separately when traveling. Bernstein wrote some of the music while taking a train to Hartford, Connecticut, where the Philharmonic was scheduled to perform. Halina Rodzinski, the conductor's wife, sat next to him and watched him cover page after page with notes. Bernstein noticed her looking over his shoulder. Smiling, he turned to her and said, "You have no idea how exciting it is to hear in one's head the music that comes out in these black dots."

The Ballet Theatre had given Robbins a small budget for *Fancy Free,* just three hundred dollars, so he and Bernstein cut costs wherever they could. They wanted their ballet to begin in an unusual way, with

Chapter Four: *Suddenly—Boom!*

a blues song playing on a jukebox. But when it proved too expensive to hire famous singer Billie Holiday, they asked Shirley Bernstein to record it instead.

Fancy Free opened at New York City's Metropolitan Opera House, a place known to New Yorkers as "the Met," on April 18, 1944. This ballet was nothing like any that had been staged before, at the Met or anywhere else. When Bernstein raised his baton and the audience heard not the orchestra, but jukebox music, people gasped. Had something gone wrong? Had someone left a radio playing backstage? Then, suddenly, three sailors cartwheeled onto the stage to the sound of rattling drums, and the audience fell in love with this brash, funny, energetic ballet. When it was over, they hated to stop clapping and made the dancers take twenty-four curtain calls.

The *New York Times* proclaimed the new ballet "exactly ten degrees north of terrific." *Time* magazine praised the dancing and

A scene from a performance of the ballet *Fancy Free*

called *Fancy Free* the "surprise hit of Manhattan's booming ballet season." It was such a big hit that attendance broke box-office records. Every night, people filled the 3,300 seats and stood in the aisles. The Met added two more weeks of performances, and the Ballet Theatre performed *Fancy Free* on a national tour.

Their big success thrilled the ballet's two young creators. "Fun? I'll say! I'm still not over it," Bernstein wrote to Aaron Copland. Robbins asked, "Who am I? Just a guy from Weehawken, and all of a sudden—boom!"

One good idea often leads to another. When Oliver Smith, a Broadway producer, saw *Fancy Free,* he knew right away that the story of the three sailors would make a great musical show, one with songs, dance, and speaking parts. Smith offered to produce the show if Bernstein would compose the songs and Robbins would choreograph the dances. (Producers handle business matters and supervise the many tasks involved in bringing a show to the stage.) Robbins and Bernstein agreed to create the show, called *On the Town,* on one condition. Bernstein insisted that Smith hire his friends from the Revuers, Adolph Green and Betty Comden, to write the dialogue and song lyrics. This meant that most of the creative team would be newcomers. Only the show's director, George Abbott, had a solid background in show business.

"We started from Square One with a totally new series of conceptions," Bernstein recalled. There were "different plot ideas, different scenarios, which we had great fun bouncing off each other's brains and souls." In *On the Town,* the sailors have names: Chip, Gabey, and Ozzie. "We wanted them to come off as people," Comden and Green explained. "We wanted them to possess the qualities and attitudes of the servicemen we had seen coming into the city for the first time and at least touch on the frantic search for gaiety and love, and the terrific pressure of time that war brings." The sailors meet women who reflect the independent lives pioneered by many women during the war. Like those who took over the jobs of men fighting overseas, Hildy drives a taxi. Claire, a career woman, works as an anthropologist, and Ivy studies dance.

The team wrote the show quickly, in the summer of 1944. "How could we do that?" Robbins asked. "We didn't know any better." The writing kept going when Bernstein and Robbins went into the hospital.

Chapter Four: *Suddenly—Boom!*

Bernstein needed surgery to rid him of chronic sinus infections, and Robbins was having his tonsils removed. They shared a room during recovery, so Betty Comden visited them to work on the songs. Even in the hospital, though, it was impossible to write without interruption. Friends kept dropping in to play cards or pass the time. As Bernstein's laughter echoed in the hallway, one of the nurses complained, "He may be God's gift to music, but I'd hate to tell you where he gives me a pain."

Bernstein had to compose twenty-five songs and dance numbers for *On the Town*. They were as varied as "New York, New York," the upbeat anthem that the sailors sing when they first step ashore, and the "Times Square Ballet," which brings many servicemen together at New York City's busiest crossroads. Every bit of the music was new. "There was not a note of *Fancy Free* music in *On the Town*," Bernstein said. He was so busy that he needed help organizing his schedule and answering his mail. In July, Helen Coates retired from teaching and moved to New York City to become her favorite student's secretary.

As soon as the show was written, rehearsals began. One of the dancers recalled the first rehearsal that Bernstein attended. He burst in like an "apparition with his coat draped over his shoulders as a cape and his hair flying," she said. Bernstein greeted the cast, sat down at the piano, and played one of the big dance numbers from the show. "All us little kids were just struck dumb with admiration and love," the dancer added.

Shows bound for the New York stage usually open first in another city. This out-of-town tryout gives the writers,

A movie poster for *On the Town*. The musical was made into a film in 1949.

45

director, and choreographer a chance to polish the show and fix any problems before the New York critics pronounce judgment. During the ten nights that *On the Town* played in Boston, Robbins reworked one of the dances, Abbott cut several songs, and Comden and Green wrote new dialogue. As the curtain fell on the eighth performance, Abbott called out, "Freeze it!" *On the Town* was ready for Broadway.

The show that New Yorkers saw on December 28, 1944, broke new ground. Popular musicals of previous years, such as *Oklahoma!*, had presented small-town America as it used to be, but *On the Town* was urban and up-to-the-minute. It offered nearly half an hour of dance, more than any show before it, and it featured something never before seen on the Broadway stage: blacks and whites dancing and singing together. The critics loved *On the Town,* calling it fresh, funny, and "a wow."

In one incredible year, 1944, Leonard Bernstein had given the public the *Jeremiah* Symphony, *Fancy Free,* and *On the Town*. He had thrilled New York's theatergoers, but he had disappointed someone whose opinion mattered more: Serge Koussevitzky. The maestro had attended the Boston opening of *On the Town,* and what he saw and heard made him furious. "He gave me a three-hour lecture the next day on the way I was going," Bernstein said. Bernstein had the ability to be a great conductor, Koussevitzky believed, but writing popular works for the stage wasted his talent. Bernstein took his mentor's words to heart and promised, "from now on I intend to stick to the classics."

By October 1945, when Leonard Bernstein was named conductor of the New York City Symphony Orchestra, *On the Town* already seemed quaint. World War II had ended in August after U.S. planes dropped atomic bombs on two Japanese cities, Hiroshima and Nagasaki, forcing Japan to surrender. With two entire cities flattened and thousands of Japanese civilians killed or dying of radiation poisoning, people the world over doubted that they would ever feel carefree again.

The New York City Symphony Orchestra was only two years old, having been formed in 1943 to play in a new hall, the City Center for Music and Dance. There was no money to pay a conductor's salary, but Bernstein hardly minded, because he earned fees from the orchestras in other cities that he conducted as a guest. He welcomed this opportunity to plan a season of concerts and sharpen his conducting skills.

The orchestra's managers promised that listeners would hear "vital music old and new, superbly performed under a stimulating young conductor at prices within the reach of all." Bernstein worked hard to present something novel in every concert, perhaps the premiere of a new work or music that New Yorkers rarely had the chance to hear.

Bernstein also invited great musicians to perform with the New York City Symphony Orchestra, including Chilean-born pianist Claudio Arrau. After a concert in February 1946, Bernstein attended a party at Arrau's home in Queens, New York. There he met twenty-four-year-old Felicia Montealegre Cohn, who had come to New York from Chile to act. Bernstein felt drawn to this stylish, smart young woman who loved to laugh. He sat with her on a sofa for hours, talking about music, plays, and books.

Bernstein had moved out of his Carnegie Hall room and into an apartment on the top floor of a building on West Tenth Street, in lower Manhattan. Felicia, who had a part in a play, lived nearby. The two saw each other whenever Bernstein could spare the time, and soon the press reported that they were engaged to be married. "She's an angel and a wonderful companion," Bernstein said.

When would the wedding take place? Leonard Bernstein was a busy man. He was creating another ballet with Jerome Robbins, one called *Facsimile*. More somber than *Fancy Free,* this ballet featured three lonely characters, two men and a woman, trying to find meaningful relationships. Bernstein was also traveling the world, conducting orchestras on the West Coast and in Canada and London. "With Lenny his music comes first and it always will," commented Helen Coates. "If he ever does marry, his wife will have to recognize that from the beginning."

Then, in 1947, Bernstein discovered a new love: Palestine.

Bernstein being introduced at a concert with the Israel Philharmonic Orchestra in Tel Aviv on November 20, 1948. Hundreds of soldiers and settlers attended the concert, which took place in an empty lot with an excavation as a backdrop.

Chapter Five
Life, Love, and the World

Palestine, in 1947, was a land of desert sand dunes, fragrant orange groves, and noisy, swelling cities. It was home to families who had lived in the Holy Land for generations and refugees from the European war who were eager to start a new life.

Hebrew tribes had settled in this Middle Eastern region more than 3,000 years earlier, but over the centuries a series of foreign invaders had seized control. Babylonians, Persians, Greeks, Romans, and Turks all wanted to possess this strategic land, which offered access to three continents. Arabs moved in as well; when Great Britain captured Palestine in 1917, most Palestinians were Arab Muslims. Yet Jews throughout the world traced their roots to this historic place, and the British promised the Jews of Palestine an independent homeland.

As thousands of European Jews sought safety in Palestine following the rise of Nazism in the 1930s, Arab Muslims protested, sometimes violently. Britain tried to make peace by restricting Jewish immigration and limiting the amount of land that Jews could buy. But after World War II, Jews were insisting on their independence, Muslims were resisting the growing Jewish presence, and both sides were carrying out acts of terrorism. The British turned the problem over to the United Nations in April 1947, the same month Bernstein traveled to Palestine with his father and sister. He had been invited to conduct the Palestine Philharmonic Orchestra, whose members were Jewish musicians.

Bernstein felt deeply connected to the Jews of Palestine, observing "a strength and devotion in these people that is formidable." The land, he said, was "beautiful beyond description." The three Bernsteins visited the Dead Sea, which is saltier by far than any of the world's oceans, and the gleaming new city of Tel Aviv, where violence and danger were part of daily life. Explosions destroyed the local police station during the Bernsteins' visit, and a British man was kidnapped from their hotel. Still, Leonard and the orchestra calmly rehearsed, and they played concerts in Tel Aviv, Haifa, and Jerusalem. Their program included the *Jeremiah* Symphony and the Piano Concerto by Maurice Ravel, with Bernstein playing the piano and conducting the orchestra at the same time.

Leonard Bernstein was used to crowds and standing ovations, but nothing had prepared him for the welcome he received from the Jews of Palestine. Hundreds of people descended on Jerusalem's Edison Hall to hear him perform there, and most had to be turned away. When Bernstein walked onto the stage, the applause was deafening. He and the musicians took five bows after the *Jeremiah* Symphony and more following the concerto. People clapped both for the music and for its electrifying conductor. "If Bernstein had played *Pop! Goes the Weasel,* the audience would have loved him just as much," reported *Time* magazine.

The final concert of Bernstein's two weeks in Palestine took place under the stars at Ein Harod, a large kibbutz (collective farm). Ein Harod was near Mount Gilboa, a ridge famed for the wild purple irises that cover it each spring. Some 3,500 people "had come by truck or wagon and on foot," wrote an American reporter; "they lay atop cars, stood in the aisles and spilled over onto the platform. It was as if Heaven had sent them this genius to help them forget their troubles."

The musicians, too, admired this conductor who spoke Hebrew, the ancient language that Palestine's Jews had brought back to life. They invited him to be their permanent music director and said they would require very little from him, merely three months of his time each year. Bernstein felt tempted to say yes, but he had to decline. The problem was one he would face throughout life: too much music

Chapter Five: *Life, Love, and the World*

to conduct or write, and not enough time. He offered instead to be the orchestra's musical adviser, to suggest music for its concerts. In years to come, if his schedule permitted it, he hoped to do more.

Bernstein also needed time and energy for social causes, such as racial equality. In 1947, not a single African American played in a major U.S. orchestra. When Bernstein auditioned four hundred musicians for the New York City Symphony, only three were African American, and none of the three was qualified. "I don't think it was a lack of talent," he said, "but something more serious, a lack of training." He called for more and better teaching of music in the nation's schools and scholarships for talented African Americans. He believed, too, that combating prejudice throughout society would create opportunities for African Americans in the musical world. "Anything we can do to fight discrimination—in any form or field—will ultimately work toward ameliorating the musical situation," he insisted.

All this activity left little time for romance. In December 1947, feeling neglected, Felicia Montealegre Cohn ended her engagement to Leonard Bernstein. Soon afterward, Bernstein resigned from the New York City Symphony Orchestra "with reluctance and sadness." A budget reduction had prevented him from developing the orchestra as he had wished. A free agent, he took off on a conducting tour of Europe.

Concerts scheduled in Germany and Austria made this trip controversial. Although the Nazi regime had been toppled, many Jewish musicians were refusing to perform in these nations, where Hitler's followers had murdered millions of Jews. No American conductor had led

Bernstein and his sister, Shirley, inside the liner America *on April 9, 1947, are on their way to Europe for Bernstein's conducting tour.*

a concert in Germany since the war; Bernstein would be the first. For him, this tour was a way to break down prejudice and promote understanding.

In 1948, Germany was in ruins. In the city of Munich, Bernstein saw starving people climbing over bombed-out rubble, desperate for potatoes, cabbages, or bread. Even working people suffered. The Bavarian State Orchestra went on strike after some of the musicians fainted from hunger during a rehearsal. The strike ended only when Bernstein's American colleagues gave the musicians cigarettes, which were as good as cash in the devastated city. Bernstein knew that some Germans—even some in the orchestra—still adhered to the Nazi ideal of German superiority. He knew that some despised him because he was a Jew and an American.

Yet he overcame these great challenges with his music. Leonard Bernstein was in love with music and needed to share his feelings with the world. While performing, he radiated joy that made every person present feel a little more alive. As his first concert in Munich ended, shouts of "Bravo!" filled the hall. "The audience stood on its feet and applauded him for more than ten minutes," noted the *New York Times*. It was a moment of triumph for Bernstein, but he insisted on conducting another, very different, orchestra before he left Germany.

The seventeen musicians in the Jewish Representative Orchestra were the only survivors of a group that had played together as prisoners in Dachau, an infamous Nazi concentration camp. Bernstein and these musicians played for some of the thousands of Jews who had lost everything in the war. The Nazis had robbed these people of their homes, their belongings, their loved ones, and often their health. Many dreamed of going to Palestine but were prevented from immigrating by the British quota. They spent day after day in displaced-persons camps. After these concerts, the grateful musicians honored their guest conductor with a treasured gift: the prison-camp uniform worn by the orchestra's founder, a flutist killed by the Nazis.

Bernstein had seen for himself war's terrible toll. He understood that the postwar world was far different from the one he had known before. Men and women everywhere had seen the horrors of the Nazi camps, where millions of people had been murdered. (Some 6 million Jews were killed during the Holocaust.) They had seen images of the atomic blasts that destroyed the Japanese cities of Hiroshima and Nagasaki. These bombings brought peace, but they raised the possibility of nuclear war with no survivors. In such a frightening new world, some people questioned whether it was possible to hope, or even to go on believing in God.

British poet W. H. Auden explored this state of mind in a long poem, *The Age of Anxiety*. Auden wrote about four characters, a woman and three men, who meet in a bar where each has come to solve a problem or escape it through drink. Much of Auden's poem takes place in the characters' minds, deep in the realm of unconscious thought. As a long night of conversation comes to an end, at least one character affirms his faith in the Creator: "In our anguish we struggle / To elude Him, to lie to Him, yet His love observes. . . ."

To Bernstein, *The Age of Anxiety* was "fascinating and hair-raising." It mirrored his own questioning soul. Melodies ran through his mind, and he began composing a second symphony, one based on Auden's poem. Bernstein wrote for the instruments of an orchestra but added a piano to represent a searching character, someone like himself.

People stand in line as they wait to fill their buckets from a water pump station among the rubble in Magdeburg, eastern Germany, on April 19, 1945.

Part One of the symphony begins with a quiet, wandering melody played by two clarinets. The piano joins in with a series of descending notes, suggesting a climb down into the unconscious mind. Part Two opens with a dirge, or lament for all that has been lost, especially the simple acceptance of God that people enjoyed before the war. This is followed by party music, which is a little too gleeful, as though the guests are forcing themselves to have a good time. Bernstein planned that the symphony would end with cautious hope that grows into certainty, and music that was beautifully full and rich. "What is left, it turns out, is faith," he said.

Bernstein worked on his *Age of Anxiety* while teaching summer students at Tanglewood and leading orchestras during a busy fall and winter concert season. He composed while traveling to Israel, which on May 14, 1948, had become the world's only Jewish state.

The Jews of Palestine had gained their independence, but the surrounding countries of Egypt, Jordan, Syria, Lebanon, and Iraq had joined the Palestinian Arabs in fighting this new nation. Desperate to survive, Israel moved troops into neighboring territory. As the United Nations worked to bring about peace, Israeli civilians remained alert and avoided taking chances that might put them in danger. Bernstein and Helen Coates experienced this caution when they flew into the city of Haifa, and their hosts drove them to Tel Aviv at night with the headlights off, to escape the notice of terrorists.

Bernstein had a happy reunion with the musicians he had befriended on his earlier trip. With independence, their orchestra had acquired a new name: the Israel Philharmonic. For two months, they traveled to concert sites with Bernstein in broken-down buses, with their instruments wrapped in blankets for protection during the bumpy rides.

On November 20, 1948, they reached Beersheba, a desert city that was the site of an important archaeological dig. The Israeli army had captured Beersheba from its Arab foes a month earlier, and although the UN had ordered the army to withdraw, it defiantly held on. An attack could come at any moment, but Bernstein and the musicians put on an afternoon concert for the forces at Beersheba. Local residents joined the soldiers at the archaeological site, where high stone walls formed a natural amphitheater. The pilots of Egyptian planes flying over reported to their commanders that the Israelis were massing

troops at Beersheba and preparing to attack. Why else would so many people have gathered there?

Again the Israeli musicians asked Bernstein to be their permanent conductor, and again he sadly said no. He was eager to get home to the United States and complete his symphony. He felt compelled to turn his thoughts and feelings into music. "The original energizing motor that makes me compose is the urge to communicate, and to communicate with as many people as possible," he said, "because what I love about life and the world is people."

He finished *The Age of Anxiety,* Symphony No. 2 (After W. H. Auden) on March 20, 1949, three weeks before it was to be performed. He dedicated it to his conducting mentor, Serge Koussevitzky. His second symphony had its premiere in Boston, with Koussevitzky conducting and Bernstein playing the piano solo part. At the time, Bernstein thought listeners could understand his symphony only if they had read Auden's poem, but in later years he changed his mind. "The Symphony," he said in 1977, "has acquired a life of its own."

With his symphony behind him, Bernstein took time to listen to his heart and discovered that he missed Felicia. "I have loved her . . . truly and deeply from the first," he confided to his sister, Shirley. "I would marry her tomorrow." He met with Felicia in New York City and asked her to take him back, but she had moved on. She was dating an actor she hoped to marry, and she was appearing in television dramas.

Felicia was on Bernstein's mind in January 1951, when the Israel Philharmonic made its first trip to America. He spent four months traveling with the orchestra and giving concerts in U.S. cities. He helped the musicians raise money for Israel and show Americans the musical accomplishments of this young country. When the tour ended, he announced that he was taking a year off from conducting to compose music. Conductor, composer, pianist—it was exhausting to pursue three careers at once and do them all well. "Sometimes," Bernstein admitted, "I wonder who I am."

In the warmth of Mexico, he started to compose an opera. He wrote not only the music, but also the libretto (words that the performers sing). Most operas have large casts and plots filled with tragic love, death, and revenge, but Bernstein's opera is small in scope. It follows a married couple named Sam and Dinah through a typical day. They begin quarreling at breakfast, when Sam tells Dinah that he cannot see their son's school play because it conflicts with his handball tournament. Sam spends much of the day at his office while Dinah visits her psychiatrist. She tells the doctor that she dreamed of a garden, where "love will teach us harmony and grace. . . . Then love will lead us to a quiet place." Afterward, she sees a movie called *Trouble in Tahiti,* but love and harmony remain a dream. That night, to avoid arguing about their problems, Dinah and Sam go to a movie— the same one that Dinah saw during the day.

It might seem strange for a man who wanted to get married to write an opera about an unhappy couple. But Bernstein was using Sam and Dinah to comment on something larger: the false values of suburban America.

Sam, Dinah, and their little boy live in one of the suburbs that were springing up around cities in the years after World War II. Scarsdale, Wellesley Hills, Brookline—the name hardly mattered, because all these suburbs seemed the same. People living there looked for happiness in the gleaming products of modern industry: an "up-to-date kitchen: washing machine: Colorful bathrooms, and Life Magazine," as Bernstein's characters sing. To Bernstein, people thought too much about what they could acquire, and they neglected something more important: one another. This was why Bernstein named his opera *Trouble in Tahiti,* after the movie that Dinah and Sam see. Tahiti was known as a tropical paradise, while suburbia was supposed to be a paradise of another kind. Yet trouble was brewing there.

Bernstein returned to New York three months later, only to learn that Serge Koussevitzky was gravely ill. He hurried to Boston and was with Koussevitzky when he died, on June 4, 1951. That summer, *Trouble in Tahiti* lay unfinished as Bernstein took over the great conductor's teaching duties at Tanglewood, which had gained a worldwide reputation for excellence thanks to Koussevitzky's tireless efforts. Bernstein spoke to the students at Tanglewood about what it had been like to learn from his beloved teacher. "We ate and drank and dreamed music," he recalled. Koussevitzky had held him to "a standard that knew no compromise, that tolerated no mediocrity." Koussevitzky had demanded the best.

Bernstein had barely settled himself in the Berkshires when Felicia came to see him. Her fiancé had died several months earlier, and she had gone to Europe to think about the future. As soon as her ship docked in New York, she had hurried to Tanglewood to see Bernstein and discover if she still had feelings for him. The answer was yes. After spending a weekend together, the two decided to marry. It was an ideal match, in Burton Bernstein's opinion, because Felicia could speak Rybernian.

Felicia, who had been raised a Roman Catholic, converted to the Jewish faith. The wedding took place quickly, on September 8, 1951, before the bride or groom had time for another change of mind. They were married at Temple Mishkan Tefila, and Bernstein wore a white suit that had been Koussevitzky's. He had also inherited his beloved teacher's cufflinks. For the rest of his life, Bernstein would wear these cufflinks when conducting and kiss them for luck before stepping onstage.

Leonard and Felicia at their wedding

Bernstein with Felicia, Jamie, and Alexander

Chapter Six
With His Whole Heart

Lenny and Felicia Bernstein took off by car for Mexico. They looked forward to a long honeymoon, and Bernstein was eager to work on his opera. They cut their trip short, though, when Bernstein received a plea for help from the Boston Symphony Orchestra, which needed him to fill in for its new conductor, who was ill. He hated to say no, so he packed up *Trouble in Tahiti* and hurried home with Felicia.

Bernstein had broken his promise to devote a year to composing. Spring 1952 was approaching, and with it the end of his composing year, but he had yet to finish his opera. He had to hurry, because Brandeis University, in Waltham, Massachusetts, wanted to present *Trouble in Tahiti* in June, during its first Festival of Creative Arts. Bernstein was to direct this festival, which featured paintings, sculptures, poetry, films, and music, all celebrating "The Contemporary Scene."

For once, music by Leonard Bernstein disappointed its listeners. *Trouble in Tahiti* sounded broken and unorganized, as though it had been composed in a rush. It "could and should have been much better," said the music critic for the *New York Times*. Bernstein tinkered with his opera, and when it was performed at Tanglewood later that summer, it was 200 percent better, he thought. Still, as composer Marc Blitzstein pointed out, the opera was "lively musically but dreary in subject."

Life for Leonard Bernstein was anything but dreary. On his thirty-fourth birthday, August 25, 1952, he and Felicia moved into the Osborne, a luxury apartment building near Carnegie Hall, and on their first anniversary, September 8, 1952, their daughter Jamie Anne Maria was born. The proud father took one look at his newborn child and pronounced her "a raving beauty—fearless and healthy."

Bernstein had also teamed up again with Betty Comden and Adolph Green to write another musical show. This one, called *Wonderful Town,* was based on a best-selling book, *My Sister Eileen,* about two sisters from Ohio seeking fame and fortune in New York City. Bernstein wrote the music for this show at lightning speed in November and December 1952. Every note seemed to fall into place.

Bubbling over with humor and high spirits, *Wonderful Town* was Bernstein's next hit. He had composed "a bright and witty score," according to the *New York Times.* The show broke attendance records in Boston and Philadelphia, where it ran before opening in New York. It won several Tony Awards, which are given for theatrical achievement, including the award for best musical. The New York Drama Critics Circle also voted it the best musical of the season.

Bernstein compared the humdrum reception of *Trouble in Tahiti* with the raves he received for *Wonderful Town* and decided that he was meant to write music for Broadway. "That is what I feel I write best, what I ought to do and what I most enjoy," he said. No doubt he believed what he said—at least at the time, because he soon went to work on another musical show.

This time he collaborated with a noted playwright, Lillian Hellman, on a musical called *Candide.* Bernstein and Hellman based this show on a satire by eighteenth-century French writer Voltaire. In Voltaire's story, a naive young man named Candide is raised by his tutor to believe that everything happens for the best "in this best of all possible worlds." This philosophy is tested when Candide is sent away from home and separated from Cunégonde, the maiden he loves. In his adventures, Candide confronts the world's treachery and cruelty, and his innocence gives way to wisdom born of experience. Candide learns that the earth is no Garden of Eden. Instead, he says, "We must cultivate our garden."

The craggy-faced, strong-minded Hellman had authored plays such as *The Children's Hour* and *The Little Foxes,* which delve into the dark regions of human nature. Writing light dialogue that sparkled with wit was something new for her. It was also a challenge to make Voltaire's story work onstage. Voltaire could move his characters all over the world and involve them in one exotic adventure after another. But Hellman had to think about whether so many scene changes could be made in the theater. Again and again, she tore up what she had written and started fresh. The work went slowly even after poet Richard Wilbur joined the team, to help write the song lyrics.

Meanwhile, Bernstein discovered television. On November 14, 1954, he appeared on the weekly show *Omnibus,* which brought the arts, history, and science into people's homes. In a live broadcast, he talked about one of the greatest musical works ever written, the Fifth Symphony by Ludwig van Beethoven. This is the famous symphony that begins with four notes, three short and one long, that sound to many people like the letter V in Morse code: *dot-dot-dot-dash.*

Lillian Hellman

Bernstein explored the hard choices Beethoven had made while composing this masterwork. He explained why Beethoven had included some musical passages and discarded others. He based his remarks on scribbling and crossed-out passages in Beethoven's sketchbooks, which he called "a bloody record of an inner battle." To demonstrate the points he was making, he had musicians move with their instruments from place to place on a floor that had been painted to look like musical staff paper.

Handsome and confident, Leonard Bernstein seemed made for TV. Many of the people tuning in had never heard anyone talk about classical music in such a compelling way. "One of the more electrifying personalities of our time" had "opened up a new field in television," a critic declared. "Thus was born a new Bernstein—television's star teacher," concluded the show's producer.

Bernstein presented more *Omnibus* programs in the months and years ahead on a wide variety of musical topics, from conducting to jazz and from modern music to the eighteenth-century master Johann Sebastian Bach. In 1956, the Academy of Television Arts and Sciences presented him with an Emmy Award for the best musical contribution to television.

By this time, the Bernsteins had two children. Their son, Alexander Serge Bernstein, had been born on July 7, 1955. "Broad shoulders and loud lungs and a glorious head and just what we wanted," Bernstein proclaimed. He wrote his TV scripts and composed music at home in his "thinking room," so he could see his two young children during the day. This gray-walled room held a grand piano, a work table, and a couch on which Bernstein could lie down and think.

He explained that a performer "is a highly public figure, an extrovert, whose whole compulsion is to get out there in front of people and let it out." A composer was different. "He has to seek out that dreadful gray solitude where he's stuck with himself," Bernstein said. "Most people of the arts belong to one group or the other. My misfortune is to live in a schizophrenic world of both."

Leonard Bernstein the performer had the chance to conduct an orchestra again. He returned to the podium in November 1956, as joint principal conductor of the New York Philharmonic Orchestra. He shared the job with one of his old heroes, Dimitri Mitropoulos.

Bernstein began his new job as *Candide* was finally headed for the stage. The new show opened on Broadway on December 1, 1956. Bernstein had composed nearly two hours of music for *Candide,* with songs for one singer, two, three, or more. The closing song, "Make Our Garden Grow," begins with Candide singing alone. When Cunégonde picks up the melody, the song becomes a duet. Soon, everyone in the cast joins in, and before long a chorus is singing, too. The orchestra rests briefly, to let these glorious voices fill the theater, before coming back to bring the song the fullest, most awesome conclusion that Bernstein could create. Bernstein had also written music for the orchestra alone, including a sprightly overture (opening piece) that was good enough to stand on its own as a concert work.

The theater critics raved about *Candide,* but Broadway audiences found less to love. Bernstein's new show was too sophisticated, too demanding, too different from everyday fare for most theatergoers to enjoy. One discouraged reviewer concluded that *Candide* bored the average person "because it does not have a romantic plot according to Broadway standards, and it does not have any songs which can be understood by disk jockeys or hung on the .... record racks of juke boxes in saloons."

The reviewer was right. Too few people bought tickets, and *Candide* closed two months after it opened. Yet Bernstein never gave up on this show. He tinkered with it for the rest of his life, always making improvements. There would be new stage productions of *Candide* in the years that followed, and the concert version of its stirring overture became one of his best-loved works for the orchestra.

Candide failed to find an audience, but there would soon be another Broadway show with music by Leonard Bernstein. This was because Jerome Robbins had another brainstorm. Robbins wanted to update *Romeo and Juliet,* to set Shakespeare's tragic love story in the twentieth century. Shakespeare's lovers belonged to feuding families, but Robbins wanted his lovers to come from rival gangs, such as the sons of Irish and Jewish immigrants who battled to control New York neighborhoods in the early 1900s. He wanted to call the show *East Side Story,* after the Lower East Side, the section of Manhattan where the immigrants had lived.

Gang warfare on the Lower East Side was a thing of the past in the 1950s, but gang fights had not disappeared from U.S. cities. Mexicans and Americans battled in Los Angeles. In New York, the violence had moved to Manhattan's Upper West Side, where newly arrived Puerto Ricans rumbled with city-born thugs. Bernstein easily convinced Robbins that the show needed to be set in the present, and to be called *West Side Story.*

Bernstein and Robbins had brought innovation to ballet with *Fancy Free,* and they were about to do the same for Broadway with *West Side Story.* Never before had a musical show dealt with hatred and its tragic effects. "I don't know how many people begged me not to waste my time on something that could not possibly succeed," Bernstein said, "a show full of hatefulness and ugliness."

Never before had a musical relied so much on dance to tell its story. Through dance, the two gangs, the Jets and the Sharks, reveal their anger and frustration; the Puerto Ricans celebrate their new lives on the U.S. mainland; and the doomed lovers, Tony and Maria, first get acquainted. Again, Bernstein and Robbins worked closely with each other, making sure the music fit the dances that Robbins was choreographing. Years later, Bernstein said: "I can feel him standing behind me saying, 'Four more beats there,' or 'No, that's too many,' or 'Yeah, that's it!'" Robbins recalled: "The continuous flow between us was an enormous excitement!"

Playbill for *West Side Story*

This much dance meant that Bernstein had a huge amount of music to compose. Needing help, he invited Stephen Sondheim, a talented young songwriter, to help with the lyrics. Bernstein and Sondheim made a good team, because one man's style balanced the other's. Bernstein tended to write gushing lyrics that overflowed with feeling, but Sondheim tried, he said, "to bring the language down to the level of real simplicity." Arthur Laurents, a playwright, was writing the script.

"Lenny never does anything in moderation," Felicia Bernstein said, and this was true for *West Side Story*. He threw himself into the project, composing music in a variety of styles. The gang members' song "Cool" echoes the jazz that was popular in New York nightclubs; the lovers' duet "Tonight" sounds operatic. While visiting his brother, Burton, then a soldier stationed in Puerto Rico, Bernstein heard the Latin rhythms that would drive the music played when the gangs dance at a neighborhood gym. Bernstein arranged all this music for the orchestra, wrote song lyrics with Sondheim, and supervised rehearsals. Exhausted, he promised Felicia, *"This is the last show I do."*

This musical was to be something other than a pleasant evening's entertainment. "*West Side Story* is one long protest against racial discrimination," Bernstein said. "That is why we wrote it." Finding a producer willing to risk money on such a strange show presented a challenge, even for two proven hit makers like Bernstein and Robbins.

Jerome Robbins leading dancers rehearsing "Cool" for the 1957 Broadway production of *West Side Story*

A number of producers passed on the project before one took it on, but she got cold feet and dropped out before rehearsals started. Sondheim appealed to Hal Prince, a successful producer with a knack for spotting quality. Prince saw four talented men doing brilliant work, and he agreed to produce the show.

West Side Story opened in Washington, D.C., on August 19, 1957. Senators, a Supreme Court justice, and President Dwight Eisenhower's chief of staff were among the hundreds of people who braved sweltering summer heat to attend. When the show began with finger snapping, jumpy, jazzy notes, and gang members in sneakers dancing a ballet, they hardly knew what to think. But Bernstein's music won them over. As the last strains died away, the audience cried for Tony and Maria, and they applauded wildly for the show's cast and creators. The next day in the nation's capital, the words *West Side Story* seemed to be on everyone's lips. The violence "is senseless, but Leonard Bernstein's score makes us feel what we do not understand," wrote the critic for the *Washington Post*.

Most New York reviews were just as glowing when *West Side Story* moved to Broadway in September: "The subject is not beautiful, but what *West Side Story* draws out of it is beautiful"; it is "as ugly as the city jungles and also pathetic, tender and forgiving." The show ran in New York for nearly two years. After touring the country for another year, the cast returned to New York and gave another 253 performances. Thanks to a 1961 film adaptation, which won ten Academy Awards, *West Side Story* gained an even wider audience. "Tonight," "I Feel Pretty," and other songs from the show became lasting favorites of the American people.

The day after *West Side Story* opened in New York, Leonard and Felicia Bernstein took off for Tel Aviv so that Bernstein could conduct the Israeli Philharmonic Orchestra at the opening of the Frederic R. Mann Auditorium, its new home. Then and throughout his life, people wanted to know where Bernstein found the energy to do so many things and do them well. "I have no more energy than anybody else," Bernstein insisted, "but I will say this. Whatever I do is with my whole heart, for the love of it."

Heifa

Petah Tiqwa
el Aviv-Yafo
JERUSALEM
Gaza
GAZA STRIP
Be'er Sheva'
ISRAEL

Bernstein, with all the power he can muster, conducting the New York Philharmonic during a rehearsal on December 31, 1957

Chapter Seven
A Double Man

When Leonard Bernstein conducted the Israeli Philharmonic Orchestra on October 2, 1957, he held a baton made of native olive wood. It was a gift from the musicians. On that evening, he said goodbye forever to his empty-handed conducting style. From then on, he used a baton to lead an orchestra, although not always the same one.

Bernstein traveled again in spring 1958, when he took the New York Philharmonic on a concert tour of Latin America. The orchestra performed in twenty-one cities, in twelve countries. The hectic schedule wore out the orchestra staff—all but Leonard Bernstein. After each concert, he was full of energy and eager to hear local musicians play. He went to nightspots where young people gathered and stayed awake for hours, dancing, listening to music, and making friends. Keeping up with the star conductor was "a full-time occupation," said the Philharmonic's harried board president.

Fans came out to welcome Bernstein at every stop on the tour. Meanwhile, Vice President Richard Nixon also flew to South America and had a hostile reception. A crowd angry over U.S. support of right-wing dictators in Latin America spat on Nixon and his wife, Pat, as they arrived in Caracas, Venezuela. Later that day, a mob attacked their motorcade with rocks, pipes, and other weapons, and enraged protesters tried to overturn the vice president's limousine. The Nixons made it to the U.S. Embassy, where they hid under armed guard until Venezuelan forces could safely return them to the airport.

Bernstein, in contrast, won people over with his music and enthusiasm, even in Caracas. "We can never overestimate the good that comes from artistic communication," he said. "When we touch one another through music, we are touching the heart, the mind, and the spirit all at once."

The following year, Dimitri Mitropoulos retired, and Bernstein was named sole conductor of the New York Philharmonic. For the first time since its founding in 1842, the orchestra would be under the complete direction of someone born and trained in the United States. As director, Bernstein gave audiences new experiences in music by bringing little-known works and fresh talent to Carnegie Hall. He announced that during his first season as music director, the Philharmonic would survey American music, playing works old and new. He was still curious about what made some music "American," just as he had been in college.

The featured composers ran the gamut, from New Englander George Chadwick—who had begun writing symphonies in the 1880s—to George Gershwin and Aaron Copland. They also included Charles Ives, whose modern music had been ignored before his recent death, and Lukas Foss, Bernstein's classmate from the Curtis Institute, who was composing piano concertos and operas.

Bernstein was offering New York's music lovers something novel and challenging, and they loved it. Younger listeners began joining longtime concertgoers at Carnegie Hall. As Bernstein's first season drew to a close, Howard Taubman, music critic for the *New York Times*, exclaimed, "What a difference one year has wrought in the New York Philharmonic!"

One of Bernstein's favorite duties as music director was leading the orchestra's "Young People's Concerts." CBS Radio had been broadcasting a few of these concerts each year, but Bernstein brought them to television. Through the Young People's Concerts, Bernstein became music teacher to the nation, introducing the children of the "baby boom," the generation born in the years after World War II, to classical music. This generation included his own children, Jamie and Alexander, who often accompanied their father to the broadcasts.

Chapter Seven: *A Double Man*

Bernstein with sixteen-year-old pianist Andre Watts after the youth's performance of the Liszt *Piano Concerto No. 1* with the New York Philharmonic at New York's Lincoln Center on January 31, 1963

"My job is an educational mission," Bernstein said, and the Young People's Concerts became central to that mission. Together he and his audience sought answers to such questions as, *What does music mean?* He summed up music's meaning as "the way it makes you feel when you hear it." He explained that "the most wonderful thing of all is that there's no limit to the different kinds of feelings music can make you have." Some of these feelings are "so deep and special that we have no words for them, and that's where music is especially marvelous," he said. "It names the feelings for us, only in notes instead of words."

Some Young People's Concerts presented budding talent. Through these broadcasts, the nation met gifted violinists, cellists, pianists, and composers who were fourteen, fifteen, and sixteen years old. An African American pianist named Andre Watts made his television debut in the Young People's Concert of January 15, 1963, when he was sixteen. Soon afterward, Bernstein invited Watts to substitute for well-known pianist Glenn Gould, who canceled a performance with the New York Philharmonic because of illness. Twenty years earlier, Bernstein had stepped into the spotlight as an unknown substitute, and now he was giving another young musician the same kind of chance. Andre Watts went on to enjoy a long, successful career.

Bernstein led fifty-three Young People's Concerts, and they were all broadcast live on CBS Television and videotaped for showing in forty other countries. Some of these concerts introduced children to the lives and music of important composers, such as Charles Ives and Aaron Copland. In one concert, Bernstein spoke about Gustav Mahler, a composer who meant a great deal to him.

Mahler had been born into a Jewish family a hundred years before, in a region of Europe that is now part of the Czech Republic. He was remembered as one of the greatest conductors of his time, and he even led the New York Philharmonic in the early twentieth century. He also wrote symphonies, songs, and other works that were rarely heard until Bernstein featured them in concerts at Carnegie Hall.

Bernstein loved Mahler's music because it expressed extremes of emotion, from absolute joy to the deepest sorrow. He believed that these pure emotions were the feelings of children, and in Mahler's music he heard "the voice of a child." In Mahler, Bernstein discovered a man like himself. They shared a Jewish heritage, and both had led the New York Philharmonic. Bernstein understood how it felt for Mahler to be both a conductor and a composer. "It's like being a double man," he said. He had the same problem, and throughout his life struggled to balance his different talents.

He was a conductor foremost in 1959, when he and Felicia toured Europe and the Middle East with the New York Philharmonic. He and the musicians spent three months in the Soviet Union, the United States' rival in the political conflict known as the Cold War. Since the end of World War II, these powerful nations had competed scientifically, artistically, and sometimes militarily to show the world which form of government was superior: Soviet communism or American democracy. Soviet citizens lived behind an imaginary "Iron Curtain." Their government controlled the information they read in newspapers and limited their contact with people and ideas from the West. Soviet leaders also suppressed music and books that they judged might weaken people's trust in them.

Bernstein went to Moscow determined to promote friendship, understanding, and peace. "Nothing else will be worth a hill of beans if we don't have peace," he said. During a concert of twentieth-century music, he turned around and spoke to the audience through an interpreter about Charles Ives. Americans were used to Leonard Bernstein the

Chapter Seven: *A Double Man*

teacher, but having a conductor address them was something new to the Soviets. Some disapproved, but most warmed to Bernstein's effort to connect. After the orchestra played Ives's four-minute work *The Unanswered Question,* they clapped, cheered, stamped their feet, and demanded to hear it again.

In the same concert, nine musicians from the Moscow Symphony Orchestra joined the New York Philharmonic on stage to play *The Rite of Spring,* the piece that had sounded so daring to Bernstein as a student at Harvard. Igor Stravinsky's groundbreaking work had not been performed in the Soviet Union for thirty years, because the government had labeled it decadent. In fact, to compose in freedom Stravinsky had lived outside the USSR, the land of his birth, for most of his life. He had become a U.S. citizen in 1946.

Soviet novelist Boris Pasternak, center, with Bernstein and Felicia in Moscow, 1959

Bernstein connected with the Soviet people both publicly and privately. One afternoon, he and Felicia drove to a country house outside Moscow to meet Boris Pasternak, author of the famous novel *Dr. Zhivago,* which portrayed the negative side of the 1917 Russian Revolution and the rise of the Soviet system. Pasternak had been forced to turn down the Nobel Prize for Literature in 1958 and had been living in seclusion ever since.

Pasternak spoke English, and he and the Bernsteins talked about art and history over an early dinner. Leonard played music from *West Side Story* on Pasternak's piano and invited the writer to his final concert in Moscow. Pasternak accepted, and by attending made his first public appearance since declining the Nobel Prize. "When I hear you I know why you were born. You have taken us up to heaven," Pasternak told his new friend. "Now we must return to earth," he added, reminding himself that the challenges of daily life waited outside the concert hall.

Bernstein also tracked down his Uncle Shlomo, who was his father's younger brother, and his father's cousin Mikhoel. He arranged a telephone call between his father and uncle, and then Samuel Bernstein flew to Moscow to hold in his arms the brother he had last seen so many years before. Shlomo and Mikhoel were forbidden to practice their faith in the USSR, and they carried cards that identified them as Jews. Leonard felt thankful that his parents had met and married in the United States. He thought about how different his life would have been if he had been born under the Soviet flag.

The concert tour continued on to the Netherlands and then to London, where Bernstein's leaping, swerving, and stabbing at the air raised many proper British eyebrows. Bernstein strived, when conducting a piece of music, to become its composer in his imagination. He wanted to experience the composer's thoughts and feelings rather than his own. For example, about conducting a symphony by Beethoven he said, "If I don't feel I'm Beethoven, I'm not doing it well."

John F. Kennedy, thirty-fifth president of the United States, and his wife, Jacqueline

One person who liked Bernstein's style was John F. Kennedy, the senator from Massachusetts who was elected president of the United States in 1960. Bernstein admired this young president, who spoke about a "New Frontier" of possibilities. As president, Kennedy would establish the Peace Corps so that young Americans could volunteer to help people in developing countries improve their lives. He challenged all Americans to make their nation and themselves the best that they could be.

Kennedy and his wife, Jacqueline, invited Bernstein to perform in a concert on the eve of his inauguration. The Kennedys asked him to compose a fanfare, a short piece of music usually played on horns and often used to announce the arrival of an important person. They also wanted him to conduct two musical selections by other composers: "Stars and Stripes Forever," a brisk, brassy march by American John Philip Sousa, and the magnificent "Hallelujah Chorus," from the *Messiah,* a work written in eighteenth-century England by George Frideric Handel.

A snowstorm struck Washington, D.C., on January 19, 1961, the date of the concert. Soon, traffic blocked streets in this city, which was unprepared for heavy snow. The Kennedys arrived at the concert hall an hour and a half late, but Bernstein was even later and had been unable to reach his hotel and change into his conducting clothes. He had no choice but to borrow a brightly colored shirt from calypso singer Harry Belafonte, who was performing in the concert as well.

Despite this mishap, the Kennedys and Bernsteins quickly became friends. Bernstein discovered in the new president "a remarkable combination of informality and stateliness," of "casualness and majesty." He said, "I think the thing that impressed me most about him, and increasingly as time went on, was the reverence he had for thought itself or for the functions of the human mind." Jacqueline Kennedy loved the arts and dreamed of building a performing arts center in the nation's capital.

It was a time of change in Washington and at home. A new baby was on the way, so later that year the Bernsteins moved into a luxurious fifteen-room duplex (two-story apartment) on fashionable Park Avenue in New York City. The family lived on the lower floor and used the upstairs rooms for entertaining. Lenny and Felicia liked to host dinner parties or have friends come over to play word games. Their third and youngest child, Nina Maria Felicia, was born on February 28, 1962.

Soon, the New York Philharmonic had a new home, too. On September 23, 1962, the orchestra moved into Philharmonic Hall (now called Avery Fisher Hall), at Lincoln Center for the Performing Arts. This brand-new Manhattan complex also housed the Metropolitan Opera, the Juilliard School, and other organizations dedicated to the performing arts. Its designers had made it a beautiful place, with a broad plaza, a central fountain that looked magical when it was lit up at night, and tall, modern stained-glass windows.

The opening concert was a festive event, attended by First Lady Jacqueline Kennedy and other high-profile people. It was also broadcast on television to the nation. Bernstein and the orchestra entertained America with a variety of music, which included a new work by his old friend Aaron Copland and the first movement of Mahler's Eighth Symphony. This glorious piece is known as the "Symphony of a Thousand," because so many musicians are needed to perform it. Mahler called for an orchestra, eight solo singers, three choruses, an organ, and extra trumpets. "It was a beautiful, exciting, memorable evening," wrote one reporter. "When Leonard Bernstein gave the downbeat," he added, "a profound emotion must have seized the most distinguished audience this city has seen in decades."

Time was passing quickly. Already Bernstein was forty-three years old with graying hair, and his father was turning seventy. Leonard composed a tribute to the Samuel Bernstein he had known as a child, calling it "Meditation on a Prayerful Theme My Father Sang in the Shower Thirty Years Ago." He also wove this sacred tune into his third symphony, called *Kaddish,* which is the name of the Jewish prayer of mourning.

Bernstein drew on varied sources when composing *Kaddish*. "It has its roots everywhere, in jazz, in Hebrew liturgical music, in Bach and Beethoven," he explained. He also returned to the theme of his Second Symphony, *The Age of Anxiety:* can human beings believe in God in the era of nuclear war? "The only theme that interests me at this point is the great question of our time," he said; "are we headed for destruction, or is there hope that man can find a way to civilization's continuation?"

Throughout the piece, a speaker addresses God against a background of music. Giving voice to the fear of death through nuclear war that so many people felt in the postwar years, the speaker asks at the symphony's start: "Is my end a minute away? An hour? / Is there even time to ask the question?" The speaker wants to recite "My own *Kaddish,*" because "There may be / No one to say it after me."

Did God create humanity in His own image, or did humans create God to fill their own needs? The speaker wrestles with this question and thinks that both possibilities may be true. The human race is maturing and requires a new relationship with God. The speaker tells

God: "Together we suffer, together exist, / And forever will recreate each other."

"What triumphs in the end," Bernstein said, is "the affirmation of faith."

Bernstein composed much of the symphony at Springate, the country home in Fairfield, Connecticut, that the Bernsteins bought in June 1963. At Springate, they spent weekends and summers away from the city's noise and congestion. The grounds featured a swimming pool, a tennis court, and a small structure that became Bernstein's studio. His family rarely saw him that summer, because he was working so feverishly on his symphony. Then, one day, Jamie spotted her father crossing the lawn and waving some sheets of paper in the air. "I finished," he called out. Felicia celebrated by jumping into the pool, fully clothed.

Kaddish had yet to be performed on November 22, 1963, a day when Bernstein was at Carnegie Hall to plan his next Young People's Concert. He was in an afternoon meeting when the orchestra's librarian burst in to announce some terrible news. President Kennedy had been assassinated while riding in a motorcade in Dallas, Texas. The sudden, violent death of this young president deeply saddened Bernstein. "The murder in Dallas was, for me, the worst experience of my life," he said. The entire nation mourned, but for Bernstein the loss was "a personal experience." Kennedy had been his friend. He knew then that he would dedicate the *Kaddish* Symphony to the fallen president.

Kaddish was to have its premiere in Israel, in December. So for their televised memorial concert for Kennedy, Bernstein and the New York Philharmonic performed the *Resurrection* Symphony, by Gustav Mahler. "We played the Mahler symphony not only in terms of resurrection for the soul of one we love, but also for the resurrection of hope in all of us who mourn him. In spite of our shock, our shame, and our despair," Bernstein noted, "we must somehow gather strength for the increase of man, strength to go on striving for those goals he cherished. In mourning him, we must be worthy of him."

Baton high and eyes closed, Bernstein conducts the orchestra in a rehearsal for the New York Philharmonic Young People's Concert titled A Study of Intervals on November 11, 1965.

Chapter Eight
Replying to Violence

One day in March 1965, singer Harry Belafonte telephoned Bernstein, seeking his help. Belafonte was in Alabama, where the Reverend Martin Luther King Jr. was leading hundreds of people from the city of Selma to the state capital, Montgomery, to demand equal voting rights for African Americans. This march was part of the great civil rights movement of the 1950s and 1960s, which Bernstein had watched with excitement. Throughout the South, demonstrators were marching, boycotting, and picketing to gain for African Americans the rights that white citizens enjoyed. Bernstein had long cared about racial equality, and in 1959 he had hired the New York Philharmonic's first African American musician, violinist Sanford Allen.

Belafonte was organizing a "Stars of Freedom Rally," a jamboree to entertain the marchers after their fourth weary day on the road, and he asked Bernstein to take part. Bernstein the composer was hard at work again, writing a choral work for Chichester Cathedral in England, but he dropped his pen and flew to Alabama to lend support. There would be time enough to finish his piece after the trip.

Sure enough, in July, Lenny, Felicia, Jamie, and Alexander were in Chichester Cathedral to hear his new work, the *Chichester Psalms*. This simple, beautiful piece, a musical setting of several psalms from the Hebrew Bible, would become one of Bernstein's best-loved compositions. According to Jewish tradition, the poetic verses known as the psalms were written by King David, a great leader of the ancient Israelites.

The word *psalm* is derived from the Greek word *psalmos,* meaning a song sung to a harp, so Bernstein composed the *Chichester Psalms* with parts for two harps. He also wrote a solo part to be sung by a boy or a countertenor (a man with a high vocal range) to represent the young King David.

The *Chichester Psalms* stands out as a moment of peace in a violent decade. By 1966, half a million young Americans were fighting in a controversial war in Vietnam, a conflict that divided the American people. Some Americans marched and carried signs to protest U.S. involvement in this Southeast Asian war and demanded its immediate end. Others called the protesters traitors and said the United States needed to win the war at all costs.

Leonard Bernstein hated all war and wished the world's people would simply try harder to live happily together. "What a thrilling world this could be, if only we knew we would never again have to indulge the brutal sin of war-making," he said. "Instead of wasting our energies in hostility and our wealth on weaponry, we could send art to the moon, exalt our Pasternaks instead of isolating them. We could feed and house and clothe everyone forever; lick cancer in a week; harness the sun's energy; learn a few languages; talk, travel, grow, and love."

His reply to violence was "to make music more intensely, more beautifully, more devotedly than before." On October 13, 1966, he dedicated one of the New York Philharmonic's concerts to the horrors of war. The audience heard *A Survivor from Warsaw,* composer Arnold Schoenberg's tribute to the victims of the Holocaust. Schoenberg had been inspired by the story of a man who had lived through the Nazi siege on the Jewish ghetto of Warsaw, Poland, in 1943. Halfway through this brief work, a chorus of men spring to their feet to thunder, "*Shema Yisroel"* ("Hear, O Israel").

The musicians and singers also performed *The Airborne Symphony,* by Marc Blitzstein, the composer who had visited Harvard in 1939 to see Bernstein's version of *The Cradle Will Rock.* This work was partly inspired by the massacre that took place in Guernica, a small Basque town, on April 26, 1937, during the Spanish Civil War. German and Italian planes dropped bombs on Guernica, killing hundreds of people. (Blitzstein had died violently in 1964. He was murdered during a robbery while vacationing on the Caribbean island of Martinique.)

"The effect on the audience was profound," wrote one music critic about the concert dedicated to war. "Mr. Bernstein came up with an adventurous program, one that left listeners with something to think about."

In 1967, fighting erupted in the Middle East after Arab nations amassed troops along Israel's borders. Israel struck swiftly and

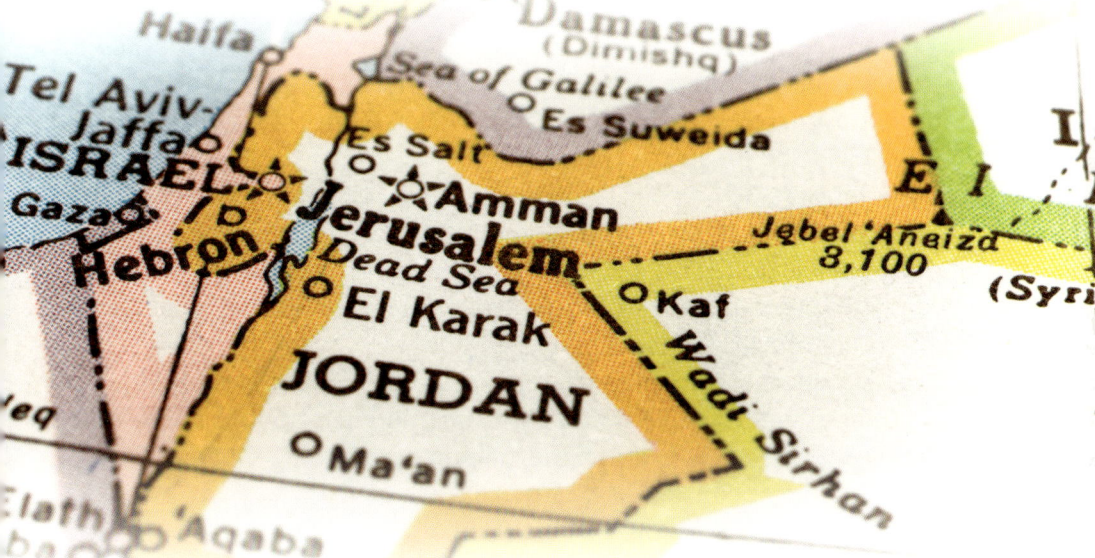

between June 5 and 10 defeated the military forces of three neighboring countries—Egypt, Syria, and Jordan. Israel also seized more territory, including East Jerusalem, which since 1948 had been controlled by Jordan. Bernstein was in Europe when the Six-Day War began, leading concerts in Italy and Austria. He donated his fee from the Vienna Philharmonic Orchestra to Israeli medical relief, and as soon as he could, he flew to his beloved Israel.

In Jerusalem, Bernstein joined other Jews to pray at the "Western Wall," the last remnant of a temple that was destroyed by Romans nearly two thousand years before. For nineteen years, this sacred site had been under Jordan's control and off limits to Jews, but the war had returned it to Israel. Bernstein entertained wounded Israeli soldiers being treated at an army hospital, and he led concerts to celebrate the reunification of the divided city of Jerusalem.

The final concert took place outdoors, in a Roman amphitheater that sat in the shade of Jerusalem's Mount Scopus. The day was so hot that the musicians played in their shirtsleeves. Bernstein selected three movements from Mahler's *Resurrection* Symphony, the piece he had conducted in memory of John F. Kennedy, to mark this historic event. He told the audience that "the ancient cycle of threat, destruction and rebirth goes on; and it is all mirrored in Mahler's music—above all the expression of simple faith—of belief that good must triumph."

Among the listeners was Adolph Green, who had flown to Israel with Bernstein. Green praised his old friend's fearlessness. Despite distant explosions and a strong wind that lifted sand into the air and knocked over music stands, "Lenny conducts with a look of almost angelic peace on his face," Green said.

Could Bernstein look forward to living in a world at peace? In 1968, the efforts of Robert Kennedy to become the Democratic Party's presidential candidate gave him hope. The brother of the late president wanted to bring the American soldiers home from Vietnam. He was committed to racial equality and help for the poor. Robert Kennedy rejected hatred and lawlessness and called instead for "love and wisdom, and compassion toward one another, and a feeling of justice toward those who still suffer within our country, whether they be white or they be black."

Then, on June 5, 1968, Robert Kennedy was assassinated while campaigning in California. Bernstein broke down in grief, and he worried about the future of civilization in such a dangerous world. But public figures have only a brief time for their private sorrow. That very day, Jacqueline Kennedy asked Bernstein to plan the music for her brother-in-law's funeral. It was to be held at St. Patrick's Cathedral in New York City and broadcast on television. Again, Leonard Bernstein would help his fellow citizens mourn a fallen hero. Many Americans who were alive in 1968 have never forgotten the heavenly sound of Bernstein conducting Mahler's Fifth Symphony as Robert Kennedy's children carried the Communion elements to the altar of the cathedral.

Leonard Bernstein faced one more great loss before the turbulent 1960s ended. On April 30, 1969, Samuel Bernstein died of a heart attack at age seventy-seven, following years of failing health. To honor him, Bernstein and the New York Philharmonic performed the *Jeremiah* Symphony. As a young composer, Bernstein had dedicated this symphony to his father, a man who had deeply loved the Jewish faith.

Bernstein himself was no longer young. His wavy hair was gray, and his handsome face had grown creases. At fifty, he had lost none of his energy, though, and whether conducting or playing the piano, he could still magnetize listeners' attention and bring audiences to their feet. German opera singer Dietrich Fischer-Dieskau observed that when Bernstein sat down to play, the space between his hands and the piano keyboard became "an electrified zone."

As a conductor, Bernstein still leaped, spun, and sweated. Yet when leading an orchestra, he "was the ultimate champion of the composer, committed to conveying every dimension of that composer," said Marin Alsop, music director of the Baltimore Symphony Orchestra. "I frequently had the sense that he was the composer for those moments, his association so strong that it blurred the line between conductor and creator." Alsop was inspired to become a conductor while attending one of Bernstein's Young People's Concerts in the 1960s. Twenty years later, she studied conducting with him at Tanglewood. In 2007, when she joined the Baltimore Symphony Orchestra, she became the first woman to head a major U.S. orchestra.

The concert in memory of his father was one of the last that Bernstein led as director of the New York Philharmonic. The orchestra demanded too much of his creative energy. There were always programs to plan, concerts to rehearse, and musicians who needed a listening ear. The time had come to step down. "I wanted to write music, and I wanted to be involved in the lifestream of music, and that was not to be found in the concert hall," he said.

Over twenty-five years, Leonard Bernstein had conducted the New York Philharmonic 939 times—more than anyone else. For his final concert as music director, he chose the Third Symphony by Gustav Mahler, whose music he had taught many people to love. He kissed the Koussevitzky cufflinks before walking onstage, and when the final notes died away, Bernstein stood facing the orchestra in silence, as he and the musicians communicated with their hearts, recalling the many concerts they had played together. The orchestra honored

Leonard Bernstein gives autographs backstage at Philharmonic Hall after giving his last performance as music director of the New York Philharmonic Orchestra.

Bernstein with a new title, conductor laureate, as well as a silver and gold *mezuzah*—a case containing a piece of parchment inscribed with sacred verses, which is affixed to the doorframe of a Jewish dwelling. With this gift, the musicians told Bernstein that he must always consider the New York Philharmonic his home.

Soon Bernstein was happily composing again. Jacqueline Kennedy had commissioned him to write a new piece of music for the John F. Kennedy Center for the Performing Arts, which was scheduled to open in Washington in September 1971. The cultural center that Jacqueline Kennedy had dreamed of for so long would be a memorial to her late husband.

This time Bernstein created a musical setting of the Roman Catholic Mass. Composers had been setting the Catholic ritual to music for centuries, usually with soloists and choruses singing the traditional Latin text. Bernstein's would be a Mass for the 1970s, with choruses of adults and children, solo singers, dancers, an orchestra, a rock band, and kazoos. It would follow the Latin text that had been recited during the Mass for centuries, but it would also include songs in English. In this way, Bernstein would combine the two kinds of music he wrote: serious pieces for the concert hall and scores for the musical theater.

Bernstein began composing his Mass with plenty of time to spare, but he missed being in the spotlight and kept picking up his baton. He interrupted his composing in summer 1970 to teach at Tanglewood and then to go to Japan with the New York Philharmonic. He made some progress in December, during a stay at the MacDowell Colony, an artists' retreat in New Hampshire, but then he took off to tour Europe with the Vienna Philharmonic Orchestra. In summer 1971, he zipped away to Los Angeles to oversee rehearsals for a new production of *Candide*.

By then, time was running out, and Bernstein was stumped. He had written many pages of music, but he had no idea how to end his Mass. Shirley Bernstein visited and found her brother depressed because he needed help with the songs. Shirley, who had become a theatrical agent, introduced him to Stephen Schwartz, a young composer and lyricist who had written a hit musical called *Godspell*. With Schwartz's help, Bernstein finished his Mass.

Mass: A Theatre Piece for Singers, Players and Dancers was a mammoth production with more than two hundred performers. It featured a central character, the "Celebrant," who puts on a priestly robe and leads a group of performers—the congregation—in celebration of the Mass. The Celebrant finds his beliefs tested as he confronts hard questions: Would a loving God allow wars? Would He let people die in accidents? While preparing for Communion, the holiest moment in the Mass, the Celebrant throws to the ground the chalice holding the sacramental wine and tears off his robe, rejecting his beliefs. Only when the Mass ends, when he announces "Go in peace," does he start to regain his once-firm faith.

"You go through an enormous amount of despair in that piece, and protest, agony," Bernstein pointed out, "and you come out believing that tomorrow will come, and you have recovered faith somehow."

When the Mass concluded, the audience at the Kennedy Center sat in silence for three full minutes before leaping to their feet to applaud. Some people loved Bernstein's latest achievement, and others hated it. The Kennedys, who were Roman Catholics, praised *Mass,* but the archbishop of Cincinnati denounced it as "blatant sacrilege against all we hold sacred." The critics disagreed as well. One called it "the greatest music Bernstein has ever written." Another compared the piling up of sacred music, show tunes, and dance routines to a "cake whose layers are chocolate, rhubarb, molasses and ham. Indigestible."

Bernstein said, "I write my music for people and certainly not for critics," and busied himself with new projects. On December 15, he conducted his thousandth concert with the New York Philharmonic, and on January 19, 1973, on the eve of President Richard Nixon's second inauguration, he led a concert for peace at the National Cathedral in Washington, D.C. Three thousand people crowded into the cathedral to hear Bernstein and volunteer musicians perform the *Missa in Tempore Belli* (*Mass in a Time of War*), by the great German composer Franz Josef Haydn. Twelve thousand more filled the cathedral grounds, listening to the music over loudspeakers.

He also received an invitation from Harvard University to be the Charles Eliot Norton lecturer, to live at Harvard for two semesters and give a series of six talks in spring 1973. These annual lectures, which honor one of Harvard's great teachers, have poetry as their topic, but the university sees poetry in all art forms. Aaron Copland titled the lectures he delivered in the 1950s "Music and Imagination." A few years later, artist Ben Shahn called his series "The Shape of Content." Bernstein accepted the invitation happily. "Everything I do is in one way or another teaching," he said.

Leonard Bernstein thrived at Harvard. He taught classes, attended seminars, and met informally with students, who included his daughter Jamie. He got so wrapped up in campus life that the *Harvard Crimson*—the college newspaper—named him its "Man of the Year." Bernstein did everything but write his lectures, and as snow disappeared from the banks of the Charles River, he confessed that he had run out of time. Harvard postponed the first lecture to October, and Bernstein settled down to work.

He had chosen a tough topic for his lecture series, the structure of spoken language and its relation to music. He borrowed his title, "The Unanswered Question," from composer Charles Ives, and he filmed musical examples with the Boston Symphony Orchestra. These would be projected on a screen while Bernstein spoke. He planned to give each of the six talks twice: first in a Harvard lecture hall and then later in a television studio, where it would be videotaped.

Ives never answered his question, and he never really asked it either. Bernstein believed that it was something like, what is truth? Or, what is the meaning of life? He suspected that the forward-thinking Ives might have had another question in mind as well: "whither music?" Where is music headed? Music's beauty is mysterious, but "it is also born of science," Bernstein said. "It is made of mathematically measurable elements: frequencies, durations, decibels, intervals." He explored in his lectures the sounds and structure of music and how the listener understands them.

As his last lecture concluded, Bernstein said that all music, from every period in history and every part of the world, has qualities in common. People everywhere recognize it as music and understand it, because humans' ability to respond to music is inborn. He closed by saying that "Ives' Unanswered Question has an answer. I'm no longer quite sure what the question is, but I do know that the answer is *Yes.*"

Bernstein returned to Harvard in June 1974 to see Jamie graduate. That spring, the Bernsteins had moved into the Dakota, a stately Manhattan apartment building where celebrities like John Lennon and Yoko Ono also lived. They bought one apartment to live in and another one on the top floor to be Bernstein's studio. The Bernsteins' new city living space was smaller than their old one, because Nina was the only child still living at home. Jamie was grown up and starting a career as a songwriter, and Alexander was a student at Harvard.

Bernstein's new friend, Tom Cothran, was often part of the family group. The two had met in Los Angeles in 1971, when Tom was twenty-four and working as the musical director at a radio station. Tall and slender, with wire-rimmed glasses and a ready smile, he played the piano and loved to read. Bernstein enjoyed Tom's quick mind, and before long Cothran moved to New York to be the maestro's personal assistant. Jamie Bernstein liked Cothran's goofy sense of humor.

The Dakota, built between 1880 and 1884, is one of the earliest apartment buildings along Central Park West in New York City.

Cothran was at Bernstein's side while he worked on a new musical with Alan Jay Lerner, the man who had written the lyrics for *My Fair Lady* and other popular Broadway shows. Bernstein and Lerner were writing this new show to celebrate the U.S. bicentennial, in 1976. Taking as its title the street address of the White House, 1600 Pennsylvania Avenue, the show looked inside the historic mansion over its first hundred years.

The new show would make it seem to the audience that they were watching a rehearsal of a play. There would be two actors playing several presidents and first ladies, and two others portraying their African American servants. From time to time, the actors would step out of a scene to comment on race relations in the past and present. Lerner and Bernstein had dreamed up a complicated structure for their show, but with two giants of the theater writing it, how could *1600 Pennsylvania Avenue* fail?

Composing a new show filled Bernstein with creative energy. Spending time with young friends and watching their children grow up made Lenny and Felicia happy. But all too soon, misfortune struck: Felicia learned that she had breast cancer. She had barely recovered from surgery when she received a second shock. Bernstein told her than he had fallen in love with Tom Cothran and wanted to live with him, as a gay man.

Bernstein had known since his youth that he was bisexual. Over the years, he had struggled with his attraction to men even though he loved Felicia and had married and raised a family. Felicia had never been blind to her husband's feelings, but she felt angry and betrayed. She spat out a poisonous curse: "You're going to die a bitter and lonely old man."

Bernstein in rehearsal for *1600 Pennsylvania Avenue* on January 20, 1976

Chapter Nine

Five Lives or So

Four days before *1600 Pennsylvania Avenue* was to open in Philadelphia, Bernstein was on hand to coach the orchestra: "Trumpets, really LOUD! Oomp-TSA-TSA! Oomp-TSA-TSA!" He said, "I've never been so excited about a show while doing it."

He may have been excited then, but Bernstein and Lerner knew they were in trouble on opening night, when their show dragged on for four hours, from beginning to end. The audience had come for a celebration of White House history, but they saw nothing to make them laugh, cheer, or feel proud. The dialogue was cynical, and the mood was dreary. One hotheaded man shattered a glass door when the theater refused to give back his money. The critics praised Bernstein's music, but they too found *1600 Pennsylvania Avenue* to be "a heavy, bloated, gloom cloud."

Bernstein's sister and his friends begged him not to bring the show to New York, but he had no choice. The Coca-Cola Company was funding *1600 Pennsylvania Avenue* and insisted that it open on Broadway. Bernstein and Lerner hired a new team of directors to trim away scenes. But the shorter version of the musical that opened in New York was no better. It closed after seven performances.

Deeply discouraged by the biggest failure of his career, Bernstein left for a concert tour of the United States with the New York

Philharmonic. With Tom Cothran's help, he chose poems for a new work he was composing, called *Songfest*. He was creating a group of songs by setting poetry to music. In September, as the two men moved into the Navarro Hotel in New York City, the press was reporting that Leonard and Felicia Bernstein had split. Bernstein remained close to his children throughout this rough period, and he took them to Washington, D.C., in January 1977, when he conducted a concert for the inauguration of President Jimmy Carter.

Always on the go, Bernstein flew to Palm Springs, California, to spend the winter in warmth with Cothran. But by February he was back in New York, alone. He and Cothran argued all the time, and he admitted that moving in together had been a mistake. Also, destroying his family had broken Bernstein's heart. He began to understand how much he still loved and needed Felicia. Lenny and Felicia took small steps toward healing their marriage; she invited him to have dinner at home with the family, and he moved into his studio at the Dakota.

The Bernsteins decided to vacation together in an Austrian castle that summer. Bernstein flew to Vienna to ready their quarters, but Felicia stayed home, planning to join him in a few days. She had back pain and a cough that hung on, so her doctor was running some tests. A heavy smoker like her husband, Felicia learned on July 22, 1977, that she had lung cancer. She never made it to Austria. Instead, Bernstein rushed back to the United States to care for her.

Felicia bought a house of her own in the pretty town of East Hampton, New York, on the South Fork of Long Island. She rested there between chemotherapy treatments, in a bedroom overlooking the ocean. In October, she felt well enough to travel with Bernstein to Washington, D.C., to hear an all-Bernstein concert at the Kennedy Center.

In this concert, an audience first heard *Songfest,* conducted by the composer himself. Bernstein had set to music thirteen poems by American poets. One, "To My Dear and Loving Husband," by Anne Bradstreet, written during the colonial period, was a tribute to married love:

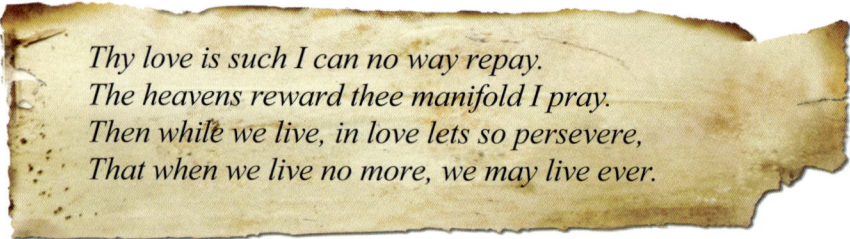

Thy love is such I can no way repay.
The heavens reward thee manifold I pray.
Then while we live, in love lets so persevere,
That when we live no more, we may live ever.

It warmed Bernstein's heart to hear the audience applaud *Songfest*. The *Washington Post* music critic praised Bernstein and his new composition, calling it an example of the "beautiful new ideas that are now pouring out of this remarkable man."

Felicia flew with Bernstein to Austria in January 1978 to hear him conduct the Vienna Symphony Orchestra, and she went with him when he led the same orchestra in London and Paris. Then, while Bernstein and the Vienna Philharmonic moved on to Amsterdam, Felicia went home to New York to resume her treatment. This trip to Europe was her last. In the early morning hours of June 16, 1978, Felicia died in her East Hampton house with Bernstein and Shirley at her side. She was just fifty-six years old.

Leonard Bernstein never got over Felicia's death. He blamed himself for her cancer, convinced that it had been brought on by stress—stress he had caused by leaving her to live with Tom Cothran. He had only barely begun to cope with his great loss when he was forced to appear in public. The National Symphony Orchestra (NSO) was staging a gala celebration for his sixtieth birthday at Wolf Trap, an outdoor music center near Washington, D.C.

More than 6,000 people gathered at Wolf Trap on the sultry night of August 25, 1978, to hear the NSO under the baton of legendary conductors, among them Bernstein and his old friend Aaron Copland. With his heart still aching, Bernstein would have preferred to spend his birthday quietly. Instead, with so many eyes on him, he had to smile, even when playwright Lillian Hellman spoke a blunt tribute to Felicia. "Leonard Bernstein will have to live with the memories of their many good times and also with those of the last horrible months," Hellman said. "Perhaps he will become the wiser for it, and these memories will lead him to create even greater things."

When it was all over, Bernstein called the celebration "the most horrible night of my life!" His fans had wanted to cheer him up, but the months after Felicia's death were a time of raw suffering. "Not even music eased the pain," he admitted. Turning sixty bothered him less. "I don't mind that I'm aged, that my hair is white, that there are lines in my face. What I mind is the terrible sense that there isn't much time," he said.

Before long, Bernstein felt well enough to stand onstage again. His daughter Nina was his companion as he traveled from city to

Bernstein, center, is welcomed as he arrives with his daughter Nina to attend a concert by the National Symphony Orchestra in honor of his sixtieth birthday at Wolf Trap Farm Park in Vienna, Virginia, on August 26, 1978.

city, conducting the world's great orchestras. Seventeen-year-old Nina needed patience and firmness to deal with her difficult father. Not only did Bernstein constantly have a cigarette in one hand, but he often held a glass of scotch in the other. He was taking prescription drugs to battle depression, and together the pills and alcohol sharpened his tongue.

Still, life had good things to offer. Bernstein looked forward to teaching at Tanglewood each summer, and he vacationed in Key West, Florida, in winter. On November 14, 1980, exactly thirty-seven years after his historic Carnegie Hall debut, he conducted Aaron Copland's *Lincoln Portrait* in honor of the composer's eightieth birthday. Like Bernstein's *Kaddish* Symphony, the *Lincoln Portrait* features a narrator, one who reads from Abraham Lincoln's speeches and letters as the orchestra plays. On this night, Copland narrated his own work. Less than a month later, the Kennedy Center honored Bernstein for a lifetime of contributions to the performing arts.

Bernstein started composing again. With help from a young writer named Stephen Wadsworth, he wrote a sequel to his 1952 opera, *Trouble in Tahiti*. Bernstein and Wadsworth called the new opera *A Quiet Place,* borrowing a phrase that the character Dinah uses to describe her dream in the first opera. *A Quiet Place* would revisit the suburban family from *Trouble in Tahiti* thirty years later, when Junior is grown up and his mother has just died in a car crash.

Bernstein, together with Stephen Wadsworth, co-author of *A Quiet Place*, meets the press in the Vienna State Opera House in Austria on April 9, 1986.

Bernstein and Wadsworth invented a complex situation for *A Quiet Place.* Forty-year-old Junior, who is gay and mentally ill, has not spoken to his father in twenty years. He has a younger sister, Dede, whose husband was once Junior's lover. This distressed family has gathered for the funeral, where the mourners include a doctor and his wife, a woman who had been in love with Dinah. Gradually the characters learn to communicate, make peace, and work toward happiness.

The Houston Grand Opera devoted June 27, 1983, to the music of Leonard Bernstein. The singers began by performing *Trouble in Tahiti*. After an intermission, they presented *A Quiet Place*. The audience clapped for seven minutes as the curtain came down, but like *Mass*, *A Quiet Place* had opponents. The worst review came from the *New York Times*, whose critic compared the new opera to "sexually candid daytime television" that "continually rings false." Another reviewer took aim at Bernstein himself, stating, "The spectacle of a prodigious talent in decline, or at least in eclipse, is never a heartening one." These words hurt, but other critics called the music some of "the richest Bernstein has composed," saying that they had witnessed "the birth of a powerful new opera."

Bernstein and Wadsworth decided that *A Quiet Place* needed more work. The plot contained too much drama; also, Bernstein's two operas seemed disconnected. They omitted the doctor's wife's love for Dinah. Then they tried mixing the two operas together, so that the scenes from *Trouble in Tahiti* became flashbacks within *A Quiet Place*. This arrangement worked well. When the new version was performed a year later in Italy, seemingly everyone had good things to say.

The Bernstein apartment at the Dakota, a quiet place since Felicia's death, was noisy and filled with life on December 2, 1984. Family and friends gathered there to see Jamie Bernstein marry David Thomas, a program director for public television. Before long, Bernstein would be the doting grandfather of Jamie's children, Francisca, born in 1987, and Evan, born in 1989.

Young people kept Leonard Bernstein youthful in spirit. He spent the summer of 1985 on tour with the European Community Youth Orchestra. The young musicians in this orchestra came from countries throughout Europe. They promoted peace and understanding through their music.

The tour took the orchestra to Japan in August, to mark the fortieth anniversary of the atomic bomb attack on Hiroshima. The day began early, with a wreath-laying ceremony at the city's Peace Park. At 8:15, the time the bomb had exploded, the park's Peace Bell was rung, and

Bernstein and Japanese conductor Eiji Oue (left), at a press conference on August 6, 1985, to discuss the Hiroshima Peace Concert. Bernstein said the concert would be played as a memorial to all the victims of World War II.

temple bells chimed throughout the city. In the concert that followed, Bernstein conducted his own *Kaddish* Symphony, and he turned the podium over to a Japanese conductor, Eiji Oue. Oue conducted *Hiroshima,* a musical memorial by female composer Tomiko Kojiba. Like Oue, Kojiba had been born in Hiroshima. For people whose countries were once enemies to come together and make music was, to Bernstein, a form of prayer.

The tireless conductor who used to stay up late after concerts, exploring the nightlife of foreign cities, was gone. He had been replaced by an aging traveler worn out by bouncing from one country to another. A journalist who caught up with Bernstein on this tour discovered a weary man. "His eyes, remembered as so alive and expressive, are empty," the reporter wrote. "Hours of flying have made him stiff. Two or more double scotches have added their toll." Bernstein spoke of regrets. "God, the number of things I have not done," he whispered. "I have a lot of music to write and this next opera is a terribly important one. I just hope I last until it's done."

Here was news: Leonard Bernstein was writing another opera. He had a big work in mind, an opera about the Holocaust. It was to be his finest achievement, the music that would cause him to be remembered as a great composer. He planned to call the opera *Babel,* after the biblical Tower of Babel. According to the Bible, God smashed this massive tower and scattered its builders to distant parts of the earth, where they developed the world's varied languages. The opera was to have scenes in different languages to show confusion, or how the people of the twentieth century failed to cooperate for the good of all.

Bernstein and Stephen Wadsworth got started, but Wadsworth quit the project in 1985. It seemed to him that Bernstein would rather dream about composing something important than sit down and do real work. *Babel* would remain unfinished.

Leonard Bernstein had better luck with smaller pieces. In fall 1986, he wrote *Jubilee Games,* a work in two movements, to celebrate the fiftieth anniversary of the Israel Philharmonic Orchestra. The first movement, "Free-Style Events," invites the musicians to improvise, or decide what to play and on the spur of the moment. The second movement, "Diaspora Dances," embraces Jewish culture throughout the world, from its roots in the Middle East to Europe and America. In the months that followed, he added two more movements to the piece and changed its title to *Concerto for Orchestra.*

In 1989, he composed another song cycle, giving it the playful title *Arias and Barcarolles.* An aria is a songlike section of an opera. A barcarolle is a song sung by the gondoliers of Venice while steering their narrow boats through the city's canals. Bernstein's *Arias and Barcarolles* are about love and family life: falling in love and marrying, having a baby, telling bedtime stories, and coping with teenage children making noise. The final song is one without words that suggests old age and the memory of past love; two singers hum along to a simple tune played on a piano.

The composer himself had reached the age for looking back and remembering. In August 1988, his friends and family, including his ninety-year-old mother, gathered at Tanglewood to spend four days celebrating Bernstein's seventieth birthday. A high school orchestra performed the *Jeremiah* Symphony, and students from Indiana University staged Bernstein's *Mass.* The birthday bash also included a night of songs written in Bernstein's honor by Stephen Sondheim, Jamie Bernstein Thomas, and others.

For the final concert, eight composers, among them Bernstein's fellow student at the Curtis Institute, Lukas Foss, wrote *A Bernstein Birthday Bouquet*. The flowers in this musical bouquet were based on the song "New York, New York," from Bernstein's first hit show, *On the Town*. Bernstein and his well-wishers also listened to selections that spanned his composing career, from *I Hate Music!* and *Wonderful Town* through *Candide, Kaddish,* and *Songfest*. About reaching seventy, Bernstein said, "I feel that I have lived five lives or so already."

Five lives or more: conductor, composer, pianist, teacher, family man, and *activist*. Bernstein still gave time to causes he believed in. In the 1980s, he worked to help people with acquired immune deficiency syndrome (AIDS). The first case of AIDS was identified in 1981, and early in the epidemic many of the infected Americans were gay men. They included Tom Cothran, who died of complications of AIDS in 1987. Bernstein led concerts to raise money for AIDS research and patient care. In 1989, he declined the National Medal of Arts, the nation's highest honor for creative achievement. The government agency awarding the medal, the National Endowment for the Arts, had withdrawn funding for an art exhibition depicting the death and suffering caused by AIDS. Bernstein refused to be linked to any group that tried to bind artists' hands or prevent their work from being seen or heard.

Bernstein is applauded after conducting an international ensemble on December 23, 1989. The East-West Concert took place shortly after the fall of the Berlin Wall.

Chapter Ten
Defiance

In February 1989, Helen Coates died, at age eighty-nine, after dedicating her life to Bernstein's education and career. He held a memorial service in his Dakota apartment for his faithful teacher, secretary, and friend.

For Bernstein, 1989 was a year of loss, but also one of love. In October, he met Mark Adams Taylor, a man born and raised in Alabama. Taylor, who was twenty-eight, wrote speeches for the president of New York University, but he dreamed of becoming a novelist. He was Bernstein's last love and became his loyal companion, often staying up late with him to solve the word games and crossword puzzles that delighted the older man.

It was also a year of triumph, for Leonard Bernstein and the free world. The economy and government of the Soviet Union were breaking down. Communism was losing its grip on Europe, and the United States was winning the Cold War. The most dramatic changes were happening in Germany, which since 1949 had been divided into two countries: democratic West Germany and communist East Germany. In 1961, the Communists had erected a concrete barrier across the city of Berlin, cutting off the eastern, communist sector from the west. The Berlin Wall became a symbol of the Cold War, as East Berliners risked being shot to cross over it to freedom.

On November 9, 1989, the East German government opened passageways in the Berlin Wall to let people move through it in both directions. Ordinary citizens began chipping away at the wall itself, and before long officials brought in bulldozers to knock it down. This was a step toward the reunification of Germany, which took place on October 3, 1990.

As someone who had spoken out for freedom all his life, Bernstein needed to be in Berlin at this historic time. On December 23, 1989, he conducted two performances of Beethoven's Ninth Symphony, one in East Berlin and the other in West Berlin. He led an orchestra of Germans joined by musicians from the four great nations that had defeated Germany in World War II: the United States, Great Britain, France, and the Soviet Union. Once again, he brought together old enemies as partners in making music.

The final movement of Beethoven's symphony features singers. It is known as the "Ode to Joy," because the composer set to music a poem with this title by German writer Friedrich von Schiller. This was the perfect music to play, because Schiller's words celebrate the unity of humankind. Bernstein made one small but important change: for *Freude*, the German word for joy, he substituted *Freiheit*, meaning freedom. "When the chorus sang the word *'Freiheit,'*" recalled an oboist from the orchestra, "I shall always remember how his face lit up."

Thousands of people stood in a cold drizzle outside the concert hall in West Berlin, watching the performance on two giant screens. But these concerts were merely a warm-up for a third one, held on Christmas Day and broadcast by satellite to more than twenty countries. On that day, Bernstein conducted the "Ode to Freedom" in the Schauspielhaus, an East German concert hall with a statue of the poet Schiller at the base of its steps. The hall faced a great public square. Many buildings on this square had been destroyed in World War II, but like much of Germany, they had been rebuilt. "I am experiencing a historical moment, incomparable with others in my long, long life," Bernstein told his millions of listeners. On that day, the East German government gave him a medal.

At seventy-one, Leonard Bernstein appeared to be on top of the world, at least when he was leading an orchestra. Offstage, the people who knew him best worried. His face looked gray and he labored to

Chapter Ten: *Defiance*

breathe, yet he lived within a choking cloud of cigarette smoke. He came home from Berlin "crawling with exhaustion," Shirley Bernstein said.

Bernstein still felt tired weeks later, after a vacation in sunny Key West that was meant to revive him. He missed the premiere of *Dance Suite,* his newest work. *Dance Suite* was performed at the Met on January 14, 1990, to celebrate the fiftieth anniversary of the American Ballet Theatre.

In spring, Bernstein became a busy conductor again, although he felt pain in his chest whenever he drew in a breath. Medical tests revealed a tumor in one lung, so he began having radiation treatments. "I am involved in a new experiment with life!" he bravely said. The radiation shrank his tumor, but it caused fluid to collect in his chest, so he had to stay in the hospital to have the fluid drained. The doctors injected him with a medication that caused a painful rash to spread over his body.

Shirley brought him to his Connecticut home, Springate, to recover, but instead of resting, he kept eyeing his calendar. It was June 16, and in ten days he was scheduled to be in Japan for the world's first Pacific Music Festival. The festival was to be a Japanese version of Tanglewood, with outdoor concerts for the public and classes for talented students. Bernstein had promised to lead a student orchestra and teach a conducting class, and he hated to let the young people down. He was so eager to make the trip that his doctors let him travel, although they thought he was making a mistake. One doctor grimly wagered that Bernstein would come home early, in a flying ambulance.

The long flight to Japan was a nightmare of pain, even with Mark Taylor doing his best to make Bernstein comfortable. After three days' rest, Bernstein addressed the crowd that had gathered for the festival's opening ceremony. Speaking slowly, in a faltering voice, he said that he hoped "to devote most of the remaining energy and time the Lord grants me to education, sharing as much as I can with younger people." If he could teach them all he had learned about music and art, about how art relates to life, and about being true to oneself, Bernstein concluded, "I will be a very happy man."

Sweating and gasping, he forced himself to the podium for his first rehearsals and concerts. "He ignores the steps which are three feet away and insists on scrambling up on the platform unaided.

It is a piece of bloody-minded defiance," noted a British journalist reporting on the festival. Standing before an orchestra, Bernstein was transformed. "His diminutive, gnome-like figure grows visibly, charged by the unfailing power of passion for music," the journalist observed. Music's power failed Bernstein on the morning of July 14. He collapsed in his room and had to be flown home, as his doctor had predicted.

Still, Leonard Bernstein refused to retire. He was determined to go to Tanglewood for the fiftieth anniversary of the Berkshire Music Center. His entire family would be on hand to see him conduct the Boston Symphony Orchestra in tribute to Serge Koussevitzky. Friends from the world of music, people he had known since he had first moved to New York City, would be there as well. New students were coming to Tanglewood, eager to learn from him, and he looked forward to a European tour with the Tanglewood student orchestra at summer's end.

Bernstein willed himself to have enough strength to lead the student orchestra in a performance of Copland's Third Symphony. "All of the old charisma was there, the radiant dedication to music," wrote one admirer; "the ailments drop away when Bernstein leaves the everyday world behind and enters into the life-enhancing element of music."

Yet five days later, on the afternoon of August 19, 1990, when it was time for the concert honoring Koussevitzky, the weary warrior walked onstage looking weaker. He managed to get through the first piece. Then, exhausted and out of breath, he handed the baton to the assistant conductor for the next selection, his own *Arias and Barcarolles,* and he went offstage to rest.

After an intermission, to everyone's surprise, Bernstein returned to the podium to conduct the day's major work, Beethoven's Seventh Symphony. The music began, and the conductor who had thrilled audiences around the world with his dancelike movements barely lifted his arms above his waist. The symphony's second movement was meant to have a quick tempo, but it plodded slowly along. "I could feel death in the music," one listener recalled. During the third movement, Bernstein clutched a rail for support, overcome by a coughing fit. His daughters watched in alarm, and Nina prepared to rush onstage to catch him if he fell. Bernstein had tried to keep his

Bernstein leaves the stage of the "Shed" at Tanglewood following his performance in 1990.

mother from knowing how sick he was, but on this day she understood that her Lenny had very little time left.

The musicians soldiered on until their conductor regained control. Bernstein drew himself up and led them to the end of the symphony—no one knew how. The audience exploded in cheers, applause, and praise for the music and its brave, determined conductor. Leonard Bernstein would never lead an orchestra again. He had conducted the first concert of his extraordinary career at Tanglewood, and he had conducted the final one there, too.

Touring Europe was out of the question. Bernstein spent his birthday in a New York City hospital. The doctors there saw no sign of cancer, but their patient suffered from emphysema, a lung disease brought on by years of heavy smoking. Bernstein's emphysema had advanced so far that every breath was a struggle for life. "I've had much more than my share of lives, of life's gifts," he said, "but I have not repaid the good Lord by taking care of my body."

Bernstein left the hospital, but at home he moved around the apartment in a wheelchair and inhaled oxygen through a tube in his nose. He worked harder and harder to breathe, and he felt constant pain as his cancer returned. Mark Taylor visited often. His sister Shirley, son, Alexander, and old friend Betty Comden came and went as well. On October 9, 1990, Bernstein announced that he was retiring from conducting. He claimed that he still planned to compose and teach, but this was wishful thinking. Five days later, his body gave out. He died at 6:15 p.m. on October 14.

Bernstein's funeral was held in the Dakota apartment. His mourners included Sid Ramin, the boy he had taught to play the piano so many years before; Lukas Foss, his Curtis classmate and friend; and Adolph Green and Betty Comden. Aaron Copland was too old and frail to attend, but Jerome Robbins was there, and so were Stephen Sondheim and Arthur Laurents from the team that had written *West Side Story*. Younger friends came, among them Stephen Wadsworth, who had helped to write *A Quiet Place*, and Mark Adams Taylor. His friends and family listened as a rabbi recited verses from the Lamentations of Jeremiah, the scripture that had inspired Bernstein's first symphony.

Leonard Bernstein's loved ones placed in his casket objects that represented the man, among them a conductor's baton and the score of Mahler's Fifth Symphony. His children also slipped in a copy of *Alice*

Chapter Ten: *Defiance*

in Wonderland. Bernstein was buried beside Felicia in the Green-Wood Cemetery, a historic, wooded burial ground in Brooklyn, New York.

The ten-year-old boy who tinkered with a used piano became one of the leading musicians of the twentieth century. He touched countless lives with his music, and many people missed him. In the days following his death, New Yorkers passing Lincoln Center saw flagpoles draped in black for mourning. The theaters of Broadway dimmed their bright marquee lights in a salute to him. On November 14, 1990, the forty-seventh anniversary of Bernstein's conducting debut, Carnegie Hall was the site of his memorial service, as musicians gathered from around the world to pay him a final tribute. They formed themselves into an orchestra and performed the overture to *Candide*, with no one standing in the conductor's spot. The man who should have been leading them was gone.

Because Leonard Bernstein lived and made music, "Young people profited for life, older ones in a rut were startled out of their routine, like-minded spirits felt that they were understood," commented singer Dietrich Fischer-Dieskau. People continue to learn from Leonard Bernstein and enjoy his music. He made many recordings, and his Young People's Concerts and other programs were preserved on film and videotape. Musicians throughout the world still perform and record his music. In 2009, for example, a new production of *West Side Story* opened on Broadway, and a new recording of *Mass* was released.

In 1943, when Bernstein first led the New York Philharmonic Orchestra, no one had heard of an American conductor. By 2008, the year he would have turned ninety, several had become well known. In that year, one leading American conductor, Michael Tilson Thomas, recalled that for Leonard Bernstein, "There was never any question of what he believed, what he championed. It was the joy of music. He lived it."

Timeline

1918 Born on August 25 in Lawrence, Massachusetts.
1932 Begins studying piano with Helen Coates.
1935 Graduates from Boston Latin School; enters Harvard University in the fall.
1937 Invited by Dimitri Mitropoulos to attend rehearsals with the Boston Symphony Orchestra; meets Aaron Copland in New York City.
1939 Directs *The Cradle Will Rock* at Harvard, with composer Marc Blitzstein in attendance; after graduating from Harvard on June 22, with honors in music, spends the summer in New York City with his friend Adolph Green and meets Green's performing troupe, the Revuers.
1940 Begins to study conducting at the Curtis Institute of Music in Philadelphia; spends the summer in Massachusetts, studying conducting with Serge Koussevitzky at the Berkshire Music Center at Tanglewood; conducts his first professional orchestra, the Boston Pops Orchestra.
1941 Receives his diploma in conducting from the Curtis Institute.
1943 Invited by Artur Rodzinski to be assistant conductor of the New York Philharmonic Orchestra; fills in for the ailing conductor Bruno Walter and achieves sudden stardom.
1944 Symphony No. 1, *Jeremiah*, premieres in Pittsburgh; *Fancy Free* performed; *On the Town*, the musical show developed by Bernstein, Jerome Robbins, Adolph Green, and Revuer Betty Comden, opens on Broadway.
1945 Becomes musical director of the New York City Symphony Orchestra.
1946 Conducts the premiere of *Facsimile*, his next ballet created with Jerome Robbins.
1947 Visits Palestine and conducts the Palestine Philharmonic Orchestra.
1948 Leads orchestras in Germany, Austria, and Israel.
1951 Replaces Serge Koussevitzky as head of orchestra and conducting studies at Tanglewood; marries Felicia Montealegre Cohn.
1952 Leads the premiere of *Trouble in Tahiti* at Brandeis University on June 12; first daughter, Jamie Anne Maria, is born.
1953 *Wonderful Town*, written with Comden and Green, opens in New York.
1954 Appears on the television program *Omnibus*.
1955 Son, Alexander Serge, is born.
1956 Named joint principal conductor of the New York Philharmonic Orchestra; *Candide* opens in New York.
1957 *West Side Story*, written with Stephen Sondheim and Arthur Laurents, and choreographed by Jerome Robbins, premieres in New York; named sole music director of the New York Philharmonic.
1958 Leads the first of fifty-three televised Young People's Concerts with the New York Philharmonic; tours Latin America with the orchestra.

Timeline

1959 Tours Europe with the New York Philharmonic, spending three weeks in the Soviet Union.
1961 Conducts his *Fanfare* and other works at the inaugural concert for President John F. Kennedy.
1962 Youngest child, Nina Maria Felicia, is born on February 28; conducts the New York Philharmonic in its new home at Lincoln Center for the Performing Arts.
1963 Conducts a memorial concert for President Kennedy two days after his assassination; dedicates his Symphony No. 3, *Kaddish*, to Kennedy; *Kaddish* is first performed in Israel on December 10.
1965 *Chichester Psalms* is performed in England's Chichester Cathedral.
1966 Leads the New York Philharmonic in a concert devoted to the horrors of war.
1967 Conducts the Israel Philharmonic Orchestra on Mount Scopus, overlooking Jerusalem, in celebration of Israel's victory in the Six-Day War.
1968 Conducts music by Gustav Mahler during the funeral of Robert F. Kennedy at St. Patrick's Cathedral in New York City.
1969 Father, Samuel Bernstein, dies; leads his final concert as music director of the New York Philharmonic.
1973 Conducts the Concert for Peace at the National Cathedral in Washington, D.C.; delivers the first lecture in his series "The Unanswered Question" at Harvard University.
1976 The musical *1600 Pennsylvania Avenue* opens in New York on May 4.
1978 Wife, Felicia, dies of cancer; celebration of sixtieth birthday held at Wolf Trap in Virginia.
1980 Receives a Kennedy Center Honor for his lifetime of achievement in the performing arts.
1986 Composes *Jubilee Games* for the fiftieth anniversary of the Israel Philharmonic Orchestra.
1988 Celebrates seventieth birthday.
1989 Declines the National Medal of Arts to protest the withdrawal of government funding for an art exhibition dealing with AIDS; conducts the "Ode to Freedom" in Berlin, celebrating the opening of the Berlin Wall.
1990 Attends the Pacific Music Festival in Japan; conducts his final concert, at Tanglewood; announces his retirement from performing on October 9; on October 14, dies at home.

Sources

Chapter One: *Music Was "It"*

p. 9, "I remember touching this thing..." Humphrey Burton, *Leonard Bernstein* (New York: Anchor Books, 1994), 10.

p. 9, "In the land of San Domingo..." "Oh by Jingo! Oh by Gee! (You're the Only Girl for Me)," words by Lew Brown and music by Albert von Tilzer, in *500 Best-Loved Song Lyrics,* collected and edited by Ronald Herder (Mineola, N.Y.: Dover Publications, 1998), 246.

p. 10, "delicate chest..." Shirley Bernstein, *Making Music: Leonard Bernstein* (Chicago: Encyclopedia Britannica Press, 1963), 17.

p. 10, "Every time he had an attack..." Burton Bernstein, *Family Matters: Sam, Jennie, and the Kids* (New York: Summit Books, 1982), 107.

p. 10, "His life's textbook..." Leonard Bernstein, *Findings* (New York: Anchor Books, 1982), 13.

p. 10, "And I used to weep..." Jonathan Cott, *Back to a Shadow in the Night: Music Writings and Interviews, 1968-2001* (Milwaukee: Hal Leonard, 2002), 193.

p. 11, "This boy is gifted..." Ibid., 12.

p. 12, "He saw that things..." Burton Bernstein, *Family Matters*, 113.

p. 12, "A *klezmer* you want to be?..." Cott, *Back to a Shadow in the Night,* 192.

p. 12, "It was a big hardship..." Burton, *Leonard Bernstein*, 17.

p. 12, "three indispensable qualifications..." Philip Marson, *Breeder of Democracy* (Cambridge, Mass.: Schenkman Publishing Co., 1963), 168.

p. 13, "lapping up everything..." letter from Philip Marson to Leonard Bernstein, November 24, 1957, Leonard Bernstein Collection, Library of Congress.

p. 14, "I do realize that there are..." letter from Samuel Bernstein to Helen Coates, June 24, 1933, Bernstein Collection.

p. 15, "Strewn around our living room..." Shirley Bernstein, *Making Music: Leonard Bernstein*, 25.

p. 15, "He couldn't read the Talmud..." Burton, *Leonard Bernstein*, 24.

p. 16, "Underwear can be made..." Betty Lindley and Ernest K. Lindley, *A New Deal for Youth* (New York: Viking Press, 1938), 195.

p. 17, "There is never a time..." Burton, *Leonard Bernstein*, 28.

Chapter Two: *The Wide World Beckons*

p. 19, "was meant to be seen..." Meryle Secrest, *Leonard Bernstein: A Life* (New York: Alfred A. Knopf, 1994), 39.

p. 19, "Editors of a college paper..." Le Baron Russell Briggs, "Harvard and the Individual," in *The History and Traditions of Harvard*

College (Cambridge, Mass.: Harvard Crimson, 1934), 46.

p. 20, "Music has never been the same . . ." Osgood Caruthers, "Bernstein, on Birthday, Leads Orchestra in 2 Stravinsky Works," *New York Times,* August 26, 1959, 25.

p. 21, "assurance and a considerable technique . . ." Burton, *Leonard Bernstein,* 41.

p. 21, "Anything that I did . . ." "Introduction," in Heinrich Gebhard, *The Art of Pedaling: A Manual for the Use of the Piano Pedals* (New York: Franco Colombo, 1963), vii.

p. 22, "Lenny impressed us greatly . . ." Seymour Wadler, "Bernstein at Camp," *New York Times,* October 26, 1990, A34.

p. 22, "I felt the fresh air . . ." Burton, *Leonard Bernstein,* 39.

p. 22, "Who is that nut? . . ." Burton Bernstein, *Family Matters,* 126.

p. 25, "A new world of music . . ." Burton, *Leonard Bernstein,* 41.

p. 25, "an odd-looking man . . ." Leonard Bernstein, *Findings,* 287.

p. 25, "I almost fell out . . ." Ibid.

p. 25, "He taught me a tremendous amount . . ." Ibid., 288.

p. 25, "With every element . . ." Burton, *Leonard Bernstein,* 44.

p. 25, "Man has a long time . . ." letter from Aaron Copland to Leonard Bernstein, March 23, 1948, Bernstein Collection.

p. 26, "become the mighty American river . . ." Leonard Bernstein, *Findings,* 100.

p. 27, "It all packed a thrilling wallop . . ." Leonard Lehrman, *Marc Blitzstein: A Bio-Bibliography* (Westport, Conn.: Greenwood Publishing, 2005), 256.

Chapter Three: *Seeking His Fortune*

p. 29, "I met a real . . ." Alice M. Robinson, *Betty Comden and Adolph Green: A Bio-Bibliography* (Westport, Conn.: Greenwood Press, 1994), 5.

p. 32, "scared the daylights out of me . . ." *Teachers and Teaching* (Unitel and Video Music Productions, 1994).

p. 32, "He was almost like a teacher . . ." Ibid.

p. 32, "I work and work and work . . ." Burton, *Leonard Bernstein,* 65.

p. 32, "bring them into association . . ." M. A. De Wolfe Howe, *The Tale of Tanglewood* (New York: Vanguard Press, 1946), 64.

p. 33, "If ever there was a time . . ." Aaron Copland and Vivian Perlis, *Copland: 1900-1942* (New York: St. Martin's/Marek, 1984), 406.

p. 33, "I did this one day . . ." *Teachers and Teaching.*

p. 34, "I will have to make it . . ." *Leonard Bernstein: Reflections* (Peter Rosen Productions; International Communication Agency, 1978).

p. 35, "There was so much banging away . . ." Burton, *Leonard Bernstein,* 86.

p. 35, "to seek my fortune" Ibid., 100.

p. 35, "superb and musicianly" Virgil Thomson, "Music," *New York Herald*

p. 35,   *Tribune,* April 1, 1943, 15.
p. 35,   "Don't expect . . ." Burton, *Leonard Bernstein,* 102.
p. 35,   "I hate music . . ." Leonard Bernstein, *I Hate Music! A Cycle of 5 Kid Songs for Soprano* (New York: M. Witmark and Sons, 1943), 8.
p. 35,   "Isn't she sweet . . ." Ibid., 15.
P. 36,   "How can I be blind . . ." David Wright, "Notes to the Program," *Carnegie Hall Presents the Philadelphia Orchestra,* http://www.carnegiehall.org/article/box_office/events/evt_8207_pf.html.
p. 37,   "people yelled and stamped . . ." Burton, *Leonard Bernstein,* 114.

Chapter Four: *Suddenly—Boom!*

p. 41,   "I'm going to do this . . ." Burton Bernstein, "Carnegie Hall Takes a Bow," *Town and Country,* July 1990, 74.
p. 41,   "The house roared . . ." Burton Bernstein, *Family Matters,* 146.
p. 41,   "prodigious talent" "Young Aide Leads Philharmonic, Steps in When Bruno Walter Is Ill," *New York Times,* November 14, 1943, 1.
p. 41,   "LISTENING NOW . . ." Telegram from Serge Koussevitzky to Leonard Bernstein, November 14, 1943, Bernstein Collection.
p. 41,   "dazzled, bewildered, stupefied . . ." *Leonard Bernstein: Reflections.*
p. 41,   "I'm very proud . . ." Burton Bernstein, *Family Matters,* 150.
p. 42,   "That's it . . ." Burton, *Leonard Bernstein,* 126.
p. 42,   "We went crazy . . ." Ibid.
p. 42,   "You have no idea . . ." Halina Rodzinski, *Our Two Lives* (New York: Charles Scribner's Sons, 1976), 249.
p. 43,   "exactly ten degrees . . ." John Martin, "Ballet by Robbins Called Smash Hit," *New York Times,* April 19, 1944, 27.
p. 44,   "surprise hit . . ." "Black & Blue Ballet," *Time,* May 22, 1944, http://www.time.com/time/magazine/article/0,9171,796618,00.html?id-digg_share.
p. 44,   "Fun? I'll say . . ." Burton, *Leonard Bernstein,* 128.
p. 44,   "Who am I . . ." "Black & Blue Ballet," *Time.*
p. 44,   "We started from Square One . . ." Greg Lawrence, *Dance with Demons: The Life of Jerome Robbins* (New York: G. P. Putnam's Sons, 2001), 72.
p. 44,   "We wanted them to come off . . ." Betty Comden and Adolph Green, "A Pair of 'Bookmakers' Tell All," *New York Times,* February 18, 1945, 1X.
p. 44,   "How could we do that . . ." Lawrence, *Dance with Demons,* 71.
p. 45,   "He may be God's gift . . ." Ibid., 73.
p. 45,   "There was not a note . . ." Ibid., 72.
p. 45,   "apparition with his coat draped . . ." Burton, *Leonard Bernstein,* 133.
p. 46,   "Freeze it!" Ibid., 135.
p. 46,   "He gave me a three-hour lecture . . ." Seymour Peck, "'On the Town's' Tunesmith," *P.M.,* December 27, 1944, 16.

p. 46, "from now on I intend . . ." Burton, *Leonard Bernstein,* 139.
p. 47, "vital music old and new . . ." Ibid., 143.
p. 47, "She's an angel . . ." letter from Leonard Bernstein to Helen Coates, December 12, 1946, Bernstein Collection.
p. 47, "With Lenny, his music comes first . . ." Gledhill Cameron, "A Woman's Touch for the Symphony," *New York World-Telegram,* May 6, 1947, 14.

Chapter Five: *Life, Love, and the World*

p. 50, "a strength and devotion . . ." letter from Leonard Bernstein to Serge Koussevitzky, December 12, 1946, Bernstein Collection.
p. 50, "If Bernstein had played . . ." "Bernstein in Palestine," *Time,* May 12, 1947, 70.
p. 50, "had come by truck . . ." Burton, *Leonard Bernstein,* 163.
p. 51, "I don't think it was . . ." Leonard Bernstein, "The Negro in Music," *New York Times,* November 2, 1947, X7.
p. 51, "Anything we can do . . ." Ibid.
p. 51, "with reluctance and sadness . . ." "Bernstein Resigns as Symphony Head," *New York Times,* March 8, 1948, 17.
p. 52, "The audience stood . . ." "Bernstein Scores in Munich Concert," *New York Times,* May 11, 1948, 28.
p. 53, "fascinating and hair-raising . . ." Leonard Bernstein, program notes for the Boston premiere of *The Age of Anxiety,* April 8, 1949.
p. 53, "In our anguish . . ." W. H. Auden, *The Age of Anxiety* (New York: Random House, 1947), 137.
p. 54, "What is left . . ." Leonard Bernstein, program notes.
p. 55, "The original energizing motor . . ." *Leonard Bernstein: Reflections.*
p. 55, "The Symphony has acquired . . ." Bernstein speaking during an August 1977 press conference, Berlin.
p. 55, "I have loved her . . ." letter from Leonard Bernstein to Shirley Bernstein, April 26, 1950, Bernstein Collection.
p. 56, "Sometimes, I wonder . . ." "Lennie's Brainchildren." *Time,* June 23, 1952, http://www.time.com/time/magazine/article/0,9171.859809,00.html.
p. 56, "love will teach us . . ." Leonard Bernstein, *Trouble in Tahiti: An Opera in Seven Scenes* (New York: G. Schirmer, 1953) 43.
p. 56, "up-to-date kitchen . . ." Ibid., 62.
p. 57, "We ate and drank and dreamed . . ." Burton, *Leonard Bernstein,* 210

Chapter Six: *With His Whole Heart*

p. 59, "could and should have been . . ." "Lennie's Brainchildren," *Time,* June 23, 1952.

p. 60,   "a raving beauty . . ." Burton, *Leonard Bernstein,* 222.
p. 60,   "a bright and witty score" Brooks Atkinson, "At the Theatre," *New York Times,* February 26, 1953, 22.
p. 60,   "That is what I feel . . ." Burton, *Leonard Bernstein,* 227.
p. 60,   "in this best of all possible worlds . . ." Voltaire, *Candide,* translated and edited by Daniel Gordon (Boston: Bedford/St. Martin's, 1999), 42.
p. 60,   "We must cultivate . . ." Ibid., 119.
p. 61,   "a bloody record . . ." Robert Saudek, executive producer, *Omnibus* III, vol. 5 (CBS Television Network, November 14, 1954).
p. 62,   "One of the more electrifying personalities . . ." "Omnibus." *Leonard Bernstein,* http://www.leonardbernstein.com/omnibus_publications.htm.
p. 62,   "Thus was born . . ." Burton, *Leonard Bernstein,* 241.
p. 62,   "Broad shoulders and loud lungs . . ." Ibid., 249.
p. 62,   "is a highly public figure . . ." Eleanor Harris, "The Happy Genius," *Saturday Evening Post,* June 16, 1956, 52.
p. 63,   "because it does not have . . ." John Chapman, "'Candide' a Fine Musical," *New York Sunday News,* December 9, 1956, 3.
p. 63,   "I don't know how many people . . ." Horatia Harrod, "50 Years of West Side Story," *Telegraph,* August 8, 2008, http://www.telegraph.co.uk/culture/donotmigrate/3556882/50-years-of-West-Side-Story.html.
p. 64,   "I can feel him standing . . ." Lawrence, *Dance with Demons,* 248.
p. 64,   "The continuous flow . . ." Ibid.
p. 64,   "to bring the language down . . ." Ibid., 247.
p. 64,   "Lenny never does anything . . ." Harris, "The Happy Genius," 52.
p. 65,   *"This is the last show . . ."* Burton, *Leonard Bernstein,* 271.
p. 65,   *"West Side Story* is one long protest . . ." Burton Bernstein and Barbara B. Haws, *Leonard Bernstein: American Original* (New York: HarperCollins, 2008), 44-45.
p. 66,   "is senseless . . ." Richard L. Coe, "'West Side' Has That Beat," *Washington Post,* August 20, 1957, B12.
p. 66,   "The subject is not beautiful . . ." Brooks Atkinson, "Theatre: The Jungles of the City," *New York Times,* September 27, 1957, 14.
p. 66,   "I have no more energy . . ." Burton, *Leonard Bernstein,* 312.

Chapter Seven: *A Double Man*

p. 69,   "a full-time occupation" Bernstein and Haws, *Leonard Bernstein: American Original,* 122.
p. 70,   "We can never overestimate . . ." Ibid., 124.
p. 70,   "What a difference . . ." Howard Taubman, "Aura of Success: Leonard Bernstein Animates New York Philharmonic with Fresh Spirit," *New York Times,* May 3, 1959, XII.

p. 71, "educational mission . . ." Laurie Shulman, "Music's Monarch," *Minnesota Orchestra,* http://www.minnesotaorchestra.org/programnotes/Jan-2009_Bernstein_article.pdf.

p. 71, "the way it makes you feel . . ." Leonard Bernstein, *Leonard Bernstein's Young People's Concerts,* 27.

p. 71, "the most wonderful thing . . ." Ibid., 28.

p. 72, "the voice of a child" New York Philharmonic Young People's Concerts #1, 3rd Season: 1960, with Leonard Bernstein, Final Podium Script, Bernstein Collection, 8.

p. 72, "It's like being a double man . . ." Ibid., 5.

p. 72, "Nothing else will be worth . . ." "Music: Cheers—and Carping," *Newsweek,* September 7, 1959, 76.

p. 73, "When I hear you . . ." Tom Lambert, "Pasternak and Audience Hail Bernstein Concert," *New York Herald Tribune,* September 12, 1959, 3.

p. 74, "If I don't feel . . ." Burton, *Leonard Bernstein,* 303.

p. 75, "a remarkable combination . . ." Leonard Bernstein, Oral History Interview for the John F. Kennedy Presidential Library, July 21, 1965, 2.

p. 76, "It was a beautiful . . ." John Chapman, "An Exciting, Memorable Evening: Concert at Philharmonic Hall . . ." *New York Daily News,* September 24, 1962, 43.

p. 76, "It has its roots . . ." *Leonard Bernstein: Reflections.*

p. 76, "The only theme that interests me . . ." Miles Smith, "New Theatrical Form: Opera on Broadway . . ." *Baltimore Sun,* January 5, 1967, B4.

p. 76, "Is my end a minute away . . ." Leonard Bernstein, *Kaddish: Symphony No. 3, Vocal Score.* New York: Amberson Enterprises, 1965, v.

p. 76, "My own *Kaddish* . . ." Ibid.

p. 76, "Together we suffer . . ." Ibid, 1.

p. 77, "What triumphs in the end . . ." *Leonard Bernstein: Reflections.*

p. 77, "I finished . . ." Judith Clurman, "Shaking a Fist at the Almighty," *The Juilliard Journal Online,* http://www.juilliard.edu/update/journal/j_articles92.html.

p. 77, "The murder in Dallas . . ." Leonard Bernstein, Oral History, 15.

p. 77, "We played the Mahler symphony . . ." Leonard Bernstein, *Findings,* 216-17.

Chapter Eight: *Replying to Violence*

p. 80, "What a thrilling world . . ." Bernstein and Haws, 117.

p. 80, "to make music . . ." "Bernstein: The Best of All Possible Worlds." *Carnegie Hall,* http://www.carnegiehall.org/bernstein/index.html.

p. 80, "*Shema Yisroel*" Howard Klein, "Philharmonic Turns to War for Theme of Gripping Concert," *New York Times,* October 14, 1966, 49.

p. 81, "The effect on the audience . . ." Ibid.

p. 82, "the ancient cycle of threat . . ." Leonard Bernstein, *Findings,* 265.

p. 82, "Lenny conducts with a look . . ." Adolph Green, "The Day They

115

	Made Music on Mt. Scopus," *New York Times,* August 9, 1967, 11D.
p. 82,	"love and wisdom . . ." Evan Thomas, *Robert Kennedy: His Life* (New York: Simon and Schuster, 2000), 367.
p. 83,	"an electrified zone" Dietrich Fischer-Dieskau, *Reverberations: The Memoirs of Dietrich Fischer-Dieskau* (New York: Fromm International, 1989), 179.
p. 83,	"was the ultimate champion . . ." Marin Alsop, "Leonard Bernstein." *Leonard Bernstein—The Conductor,* http://www.leonardbernstein.com/conductor.htm.
p. 83,	"I wanted to write music . . ." "Leonard Bernstein: An Exclusive Interview," *ASCAP Today,* July 1972, 10.
p. 86,	"You go through . . ." Ibid., 11.
p. 86,	"blatant sacrilege . . ." "The Talk of the Town: *Mass*," *New Yorker,* June 10, 1972, 25.
p. 86,	"the greatest music . . ." Paul Hume, "Bernstein's Mass: 'A Reaffirmation of Faith,'" *Washington Post,* September 9, 1971, C3.
p. 86,	"cake whose layers are . . ." John Simon, "'Mass' Hysteria," *New York,* July 17, 1972. 46.
p. 86,	"I write my music . . ." *Leonard Bernstein: Reflections.*
p. 87,	"Everything I do . . ." "Leonard Bernstein: An Exclusive Interview," 7.
p. 87,	"whither music?" Leonard Bernstein, *The Unanswered Question: Six Talks at Harvard* (Cambridge, Mass.: Harvard University Press, 1976), 5.
p. 87,	"It is also born of . . ." Ibid., 9.
p. 87,	"Ives' Unanswered Question . . ." Ibid., 425.
p. 89,	"You're going to die . . ." Burton, *Leonard Bernstein,* 447.

Chapter Nine: *Five Lives or So*

p. 91,	"Trumpets, really LOUD . . ." William B. Collins, "Bernstein Has a Good Feeling about '1600,'" *Philadelphia Inquirer,* February 22, 1976, H-1.
p. 91,	"I've never been so excited . . ." Ibid.
p. 91,	"a heavy, bloated, gloom cloud . . ." William B. Collins, "Giants of the Stage Produce a Puny '1600,'" *Philadelphia Inquirer,* February 22, 1976, 3-D.
p. 92,	"Thy love is such . . ." Joseph R. McElrath, Jr., and Allan P. Robb, eds. *The Complete Works of Anne Bradstreet* (Boston: Twayne, 1981), 180.
p. 93,	"beautiful new ideas . . ." Paul Hume, "All Hail 'Slava,' with Bernstein Razzmatazz," *Washington Post,* October 12, 1977, B1.
p. 93,	"Leonard Bernstein will have to live . . ." Burton, *Leonard Bernstein,* 452.
p. 93,	"the most horrible night . . ." Betty Dietz Krebs, "Bernstein Back in Music Mainstream," *Dayton Daily News,* April 1, 1979, 13-B.

p. 93, "Not even music . . ." Ibid.
p. 93, "I don't mind that I'm aged . . ." James Roos, "Bernstein at 60: He's a Musical Lion in Winter," *Miami Herald,* August 27, 1978, 1L.

p. 96, "sexually candid daytime television" Donal Henahan, "Opera: Bernstein's 'Quiet Place' Opens in Houston," *New York Times,* June 20, 1983, C13.
p. 96, "continually rings false" Ibid.
p. 96, "The spectacle of a prodigious talent . . ." Alan Rich, "Lenny's Soap Opera," *Newsweek,* June 27, 1983, 97.
p. 96, "the richest Bernstein has composed" Andrew Porter, "Musical Events: Harmony and Grace," *New Yorker,* July 11, 1983, 88.
p. 96, "the birth of a powerful new opera . . ." Leighton Kerner, "Truth in Tahiti," *Village Voice,* July 5, 1983, 79.
p. 97, "His eyes, remembered as so alive . . ." Burton, *Leonard Bernstein,* 481.
p. 97, "God, the number of things . . ." Ibid., 482.
p. 99, "I feel that I have lived . . ." Leonard Bernstein, "Beauty and Truth Revisited," *New York Times,* August 21, 1988, II, 23.

Chapter Ten: *Defiance*

p. 102, "When the chorus sang . . ." Bernard Holland, "Remembering a Musician's Musician," *New York Times,* October 16, 1990, 28.
p. 102, "I am experiencing . . ." "Upheaval in the East: Berlin; Near the Wall, Bernstein Leads an Ode to Freedom," *New York Times,* December 26, 1989, 19.
p. 103, "I am involved in a new experiment . . ." "Leonard Bernstein," *London Daily Telegraph,* October 16, 1990, 19.
p. 103, "to devote most of the remaining energy . . ." Burton, *Leonard Bernstein,* 517.
p. 103-104, "He ignores the steps . . ." Lesley Garner, "Baton Charge," *London Sunday Telegraph,* July 15, 1990, Review 1.
p. 104, "All of the old charisma . . ." Richard Dyer, "Bernstein Brings Excitement to Tanglewood," *Boston Globe,* August 16, 1990, 78.
p. 104, "I could feel death . . ." Secrest, *Leonard Bernstein: A Life,* 409.
p. 106, "I've had much more . . ." Garner, "Baton Charge," Review 1.
p. 107, "Young people profited . . ." Fischer-Dieskau, *Reverberations: The Memoirs of Dietrich Fischer-Dieskau,* 178-179.
p. 107, "There was never any question . . ." Michael Tilson Thomas, "Performance of His Life: He Composed Himself . . ." *New York Times,* September 19, 2008, 25AR.

Bibliography

Books

Auden, W. H. *The Age of Anxiety.* New York: Random House, 1947.

Bernstein, Burton. *Family Matters: Sam, Jennie, and the Kids.* New York: Summit Books, 1982.

Bernstein, Burton, and Barbara B. Haws. *Leonard Bernstein: American Original.* New York: HarperCollins, 2008.

Bernstein, Leonard. *Findings.* New York: Anchor Books, 1982.

Bernstein, Shirley. *Making Music: Leonard Bernstein.* Chicago: Encyclopedia Britannica Press, 1963.

Burton, Humphrey. *Leonard Bernstein.* New York: Anchor Books, 1994.

Copland, Aaron, and Vivian Perlis. *Copland: 1900-1942.* New York: St. Martin's/Marek, 1984.

Cott, Jonathan. *Back to a Shadow in the Night: Music Writings and Interviews, 1968-2001.* Milwaukee: Hal Leonard, 2002.

Fischer-Dieskau, Dietrich. *Reverberations.* New York: Fromm International, 1989.

Gebhard, Heinrich. *The Art of Pedaling: A Manual for the Use of the Piano Pedals.* New York: Franco Colombo, 1963.

Herder, Ronald, ed. *500 Best-Loved Song Lyrics.* Mineola, N.Y.: Dover Publications, 1998.

The History and Traditions of Harvard College. Cambridge, Mass.: Harvard Crimson, 1934.

Howe, M. A. De Wolfe. *The Tale of Tanglewood.* New York: Vanguard Press, 1946.

Lawrence, Greg. *Dance with Demons: The Life of Jerome Robbins.* New York: G. P. Putnam's Sons, 2001.

Lehrman, Leonard. *Marc Blitzstein: A Bio-Bibliography.* Westport, Conn.: Greenwood Publishing, 2005.

Lindley, Betty, and Ernest K. Lindley. *A New Deal for Youth.* New York: Viking Press, 1938.

Marson, Philip. *Breeder of Democracy.* Cambridge, Mass.: Schenkman Publishing Co., 1963.

Robinson, Alice M. *Betty Comden and Adolph Green: A Bio-Bibliography.* Westport, Conn.: Greenwood Press, 1994.

Rodzinski, Halina. *Our Two Lives.* New York: Charles Scribner's Sons, 1976.

Secrest, Meryle. *Leonard Bernstein: A Life.* New York: Alfred A. Knopf, 1994.

Voltaire. *Candide.* Daniel Gordon, trans. and ed. Boston: Bedford/St.Martin's, 1999.

Newspapers and Periodicals
Atkinson, Brooks. "At the Theatre." *New York Times* (February 26, 1953), 22.
———. "Theatre: The Jungles of the City." *New York Times* (September 27, 1957), 14.
Bernstein, Burton. "Carnegie Hall Takes a Bow." *Town and Country* 144, no. 5122 (July 1990), 69-80.
Bernstein, Leonard. "Beauty and Truth Revisited." *New York Times* (August 21, 1988), Sec. II, 23.
———. "The Negro in Music." *New York Times* (November 2, 1947), X7.
"Bernstein in Palestine." *Time* (May 12, 1970), 70.
"Bernstein Resigns as Symphony Head." *New York Times* (March 8, 1948), 17.
"Bernstein Scores in Munich Concert." *New York Times* (May 11, 1948), 28.
Cameron, Glendhill. "A Woman's Touch for the Symphony." *New York World-Telegram* (May 6, 1947), 14.
Caruthers, Osgood. "Bernstein, on Birthday, Leads Orchestra in 2 Stravinsky Works." *New York Times* (August 26, 1959), 25.
Chapman, John. "'Candide' a Fine Musical." *New York Sunday News* (December 9, 1956), 3.
———."An Exciting, Memorable Evening: Concert at Philharmonic Hall." *New York Daily News* (September 4, 1962), 43.
Coe, Richard L. "'West Side' Has That Beat." *Washington Post* (August 20, 1957), B12.
Collins, William B. "Bernstein Has a Good Feeling about '1600.'" *Philadelphia Inquirer* (February 22, 1976), 1-H, 4-H.
———. "Giants of the Stage Produce a Puny '1600.'" *Philadelphia Inquirer* (February 27, 1976), 3-D.
Comden, Betty, and Adolph Green. "A Pair of 'Bookmakers' Tell All." *New York Times* (February 18, 1956), 1X.
Dyer, Richard. "Bernstein Brings Excitement to Tanglewood." *Boston Globe* (August 16, 1990), 78.
Garner, Lesley. "Baton Charge." *London Sunday Telegraph* (July 15, 1990), Review 1-2.
Green, Adolph. "The Day They Made Music on Mt. Scopus." *New York Times* (August 6, 1967), 11D-12D.
Harris, Eleanor. "The Happy Genius." *Saturday Evening Post* (June 16, 1956), 40-41, 52, 55-56.
Henahan, Donal. "Opera: Bernstein's 'Quiet Place' Opens in Houston." *New York Times* (June 20, 1983), C13.
Hume, Paul. "All Hail 'Slava,' with Bernstein Razzmatazz." *Washington Post* (October 12, 1977), B1, B4.

———. "Bernstein's Mass: 'A Reaffirmation of Faith.'" *Washington Post* (September 9, 1971), A1, C3.
Kerner, Leighton. "Truth in Tahiti." *Village Voice* (July 5, 1983), 79.
Klein, Howard. "Philharmonic Turns to War for Theme of Gripping Concert." *New York Times* (October 14, 1966), 49.
Krebs, Betty Dietz. "Bernstein Back in Music Mainstream." *Dayton Daily News* (April 1, 1979), 13-B.
Lambert, Tom. "Pasternak and Audience Hail Bernstein Concert." *New York Herald Tribune* (September 12, 1959), 3.
"Leonard Bernstein." *London Daily Telegraph* (October 16, 1990), 19.
Martin, John. "Ballet by Robbins Called Smash Hit." *New York Times* (April 19, 1944), 27.
"Music: Cheers—and Carping." *Newsweek* (September 7, 1959), 76.
Peck, Seymour. "'On the Town's' Tunesmith." *P.M.* (December 27, 1944), 16.
Porter, Andrew. "Harmony and Grace." *New Yorker* (July 11, 1983), 88-89.
Rich, Alan. "Lenny's Soap Opera." *Newsweek* (June 27, 1983), 97.
Roos, James. "Bernstein at 60: He's a Musical Lion in Winter." *Miami Herald* (August 27, 1968), 1L, 21L.
Simon, John. "'Mass' Hysteria." *New York* (July 17, 1972), 46.
Smith, Miles. "New Theatrical Form: Opera on Broadway." *Baltimore Sun* (January 5, 1967), B4.
"The Talk of the Town: *Mass.*" *New Yorker* (June 10, 1972), 25-27.
Taubman, Howard. "Aura of Success: Leonard Bernstein Animates New York Philharmonic with Fresh Spirit." *New York Times* (May 3, 1959), X11.
Thomas, Michael Tilson. "Performance of His Life: He Composed Himself." *New York Times,* September 21, 2008, 1AR, 25AR.
Thomson, Virgil. "Music." *New York Herald Tribune* (April 1, 1943), 15.
Wadler, Seymour. "Bernstein at Camp." *New York Times* (October 26, 1990), A34.
"Young Aide Leads Philharmonic, Steps In When Bruno Walter Is Ill." *New York Times* (November 15, 1943), 1, 40.

Musical Scores

Bernstein, Leonard. *I Hate Music! A Cycle of 5 Kid Songs for Soprano.* New York: M. Witmark and Sons, 1943.
———. *Kaddish: Symphony No. 3, Vocal Score.* New York: Amberson Enterprises, 1965.
———. *Trouble in Tahiti: An Opera in Seven Scenes.* New York: G. Schirmer, 1953.

Online Sources

"Black & Blue Ballet." *Time,* May 22, 1944. http://www.time.com/time/magazine/article/0,9171,796618,00.html?id-digg_share.

Clurman, Judith. "Shaking a Fist at the Almighty." *The Juilliard Journal Online.* http://www.juilliard.edu/update/journal/j_articles92.html.

Harrod, Horatia. "50 Years of West Side Story." *Telegraph,* August 8, 2008. http://www.telegraph.co.uk/culture/donotmigrate/3556882/50-years-of-West-Side-Story.html.

"Lennie's Brainchildren." *Time* (June 23, 1952). http://www.time.com/time/magazine/article/0,9171.859809,00.html.

"Omnibus." *Leonard Bernstein Office.* http://www.leonardbernstein.com/omnibus_publications.htm.

Wright, David. "Notes to the Program.: *Carnegie Hall Presents the Philadelphia Orchestra, January 22, 2008.* http://www.carnegiehall.org/article/box_office/events/evt_8207_pf.html.

Shulman. "Music's Monarch." *Minnesota Orchestra.* http://www.minnesotaorchestra.org/programnotes/Jan-2009_Bernstein_article.pdf.

Web Sites

http://memory.loc.gov/ammem/collections/bernstein
The Leonard Bernstein Collection is one of the largest and most varied of the many special collections held by the Library of Congress Music Division. Its more than 400,000 items, including music and literary manuscripts, correspondence, photographs, audio and video recordings, fan mail, and other types of materials extensively document Bernstein's extraordinary life and career. The eighty-five images in the collection span almost his entire life, including one of Bernstein at age three, and there are 177 scripts from the Young People's Concerts.

http://leonardbernstein.com
A site devoted to the works and career of the composer. Among other features on the site, you can listen to Bernstein discuss studying conducting with Serge Koussevitsky and Fritz Reiner.

www.classicalnotes.net/features/bernstein.html
This site features a lengthy article titled "Leonard Bernstein. A Total Embrace of Music," which covers Bernstein's early years, influences, first RCA recordings, writing and teaching, and much more.

The Major Works

Music for the Concert Hall
I Hate Music! (1943)
Symphony No. 1: Jeremiah (1944)
Three Dance Variations from Fancy Free (1946)
Three Dance Episodes from On the Town (1947)
Symphony No. 2: The Age of Anxiety (1949)
Prelude, Fugue, and Riffs (1949)
Serenade for Solo Violin, Strings, Harp, and Percussion (1954)
Symphonic Dances from West Side Story (1961)
Symphony No. 3: Kaddish (1963)
Chichester Psalms (1965)
Songfest (1977)
Divertimento for Orchestra (1980)
Halil (1981)
Jubilee Games (1986)
Arias and Barcarolles (1988)
Missa Brevis (1988)
Dance Suite (1988)
Concerto for Orchestra (1989)

Operas
Trouble in Tahiti (1952)
A Quiet Place (1983)

Ballets
Fancy Free (1944)
Facsimile (1946)
Dybbuk (1974)

Theatrical Works
On the Town (1944)
Wonderful Town (1953)
Candide (1956)
West Side Story (1957)
Mass (1971)
1600 Pennsylvania Avenue (1976)

Books
Leonard Bernstein published several books.
The Joy of Music. New York: Simon and Schuster, 1959.
Leonard Bernstein's Young People's Concerts. New York: Simon and Schuster, 1962.
The Infinite Variety of Music. New York: Simon and Schuster, 1966.
The Unanswered Question: Six Talks at Harvard. Cambridge, Mass.: Harvard University Press, 1976.
Findings. New York: Simon and Schuster, 1982.

Index

Americans as conductors, 31, 33, 34, 39, 41, 51–52, 70, 107

Bernstein, Alexander Serge (son), 62, 70, 79, 88, 106
Bernstein, Burton (brother), 11, 13, 34, 37, 64
Bernstein, Felicia Montealegre Cohn (wife), 47, 51, 55–57, *58,* 59–60, 62, 64, 72–73, 79, 89, 93
Bernstein, Jennie (mother), 9–10, *11,* 14, 15, 34, 37, 98, 105–106
Bernstein, Leonard, *2, 8, 11, 18, 28, 33, 38, 40, 48, 51,* 57, *58,* 68, *71,* 73, *78, 84, 90, 94, 95, 97, 100, 105*
    bisexuality, 34, 89, 92, 101–102
    and the Boston Symphony Orchestra, 50, 87, 104
    childhood and youth, 9–16
    composing, 21, 29–30
    at Curtis School of Music, 31–34
    death, 106–107
    at Harvard, 19–21, 23, 26–27
    health, 10, 31, 35, 45, 95, 102–104, 106
    honors and awards, 60, 62, 86–87, 95, 99
    and the Israel Philharmonic Orchestra, 54, 56, 66, 69, 98
    as a Jew, 10, 13, 19, 34, 52, 74, 76
    later years, 93, 95, 98
    legacy, 107
    marriage and relationships, 57, 89, 92–93, 101
    in the Middle East, 49–51, 54–55
    and the New York City Symphony Orchestra, 46–47, 51
    and the New York Philharmonic Orchestra, 36–37, 39, 41, 60–62, 69–70, 83, 85–86, 107
    praise for his work, 37, 41, 43, 50, 66, 83
    as a social activist, 20, 25–26, 56, 72, 76, 80–82, 99
    style and energy, 26, 33, 66, 69, 72–74, 83, 104
    at Tanglewood, 32–34, 54–55, 57, 83–85, 95, 98, 104, 106
    television appearances, 61–62, 70–72, 76
    touring, 51–52, 72–74, 85, 96, 102
    works
        The Age of Anxiety, 53–55, 76
        Arias and Barcarolles, 98, 104
        Babel, 98
        Candide, 60, 62–63, 85, 99, 107
        Chichester Psalms, 79–80
        Cradle Will Rock, 80
        Dance Suite, 103

  Facsimile, 46
  Fancy Free, 42, *43,* 44, 46, 63
  I Hate Music!, 35, 99
  Jeremiah Symphony, 35–36, 41–42, 46, 49, 83, 98
  Jubilee Games, 98
  Kaddish, 76–77, 95, 97, 99
  Mass, 85–86, 98, 107
  1600 Pennsylvania Avenue, 88–89, 91
  A Quiet Place, 95–96
  Songfest, 92, 99
  On the Town, 44–46, *45,* 99
  Trouble in Tahiti, 56–57, 59–60, 95–96
  West Side Story, 63–66, *64, 65,* 107
  Wonderful Town, 59, 99
Bernstein, Nina Felicia (daughter), 75, 87, 93, *94,* 95, 104
Bernstein, Samuel (father), 9–16, 22, 31, 34–35, 37, 41, 49–50, 74, 76, 82–83
Bernstein, Shirley (sister), 11, 13–15, 26, 34, 37, 43, 49–50, *51,* 55, 85, 93, 103, 106
Blitzstein, Marc, 26–27, *27,* 59, 80–81
Boston Symphony Orchestra, 21, 32, 59, 104

Coates, Helen, 14, 32, 45, 47, 54, 101
Comden, Betty, *28,* 29, 44–46, 60, 106
Copland, Aaron, 23, *24,* 25, 27, 31, 32, 34–35, 70–71, 76, 86, 93, 95, 106
Cothran, Tom, 88–89, 92–93, 99
Curtis Institute of Music, *30,* 31–32, 34

Foss, Lukas, 32, 70, 99, 106

Gebhard, Heinrich, 14, 21, 23
Gershwin, George, 12, 22, 70
Green, Adolph, 22, 27, *28,* 29–30, 44, 46, 60, 82, 106

John F. Kennedy Center for the Performing Arts, 85, 86, 92, 95

Kennedy, Jacqueline, *74,* 74–76, 82, 85, 86
Kennedy, John, *74,* 74–75, 77, 82, 86
Koussevitzky, Serge, *16–17, 17,* 31–33, *33,* 34, 46, 55, 57, 104

Laurents, Arthur, 64, 106
Lerner, Alan Jay, 88–89
Lincoln Center for the Performing Arts, 75

Mahler, Gustav, 72, 76–77, 82–83, 106
Mitropoulos, Dimitri, 21–22, 27, 30–31, 33, 62, 69–70

National Symphony Orchestra, 93
New York Philharmonic Orchestra, 36, 39, 69–70, 72, 75, 107

Palestine Philharmonic Orchestra, 50
Pasternak, Boris, *73*, 73–74, 80

race and music, 26, 51–52, 79, 88–89
Reiner, Fritz, 31–32, 33
Robbins, Jerome, *28*, 42, 44–47, 63–65, *67*, 106
Rodzinski, Artur, 36–37

Sondheim, Stephen, 64–66, 98, 106
Stravinsky, Igor, *20*, 73

Taylor, Mark Adams, 101, 106
Thomas, Jamie Anne Bernstein (daughter), 60, 70, 79, 87–88, 96, 98, 104

Wadsworth, Stephen, *95*, 95–96, 98, 106
Walter, Bruno, 31, 37, 39
Watts, Andre, 71, *71*
Wilbur, Richard, 60–61

Young People's Concerts, 70–72, 77, 107

Credits

All images used in this book that are not in the public domain are credited in the listing that follows:

2	Courtesy of Library of Congress
8	Courtesy of Library of Congress, Music Division
11	Courtesy of Library of Congress
13	Used under license from iStockphoto.com
15	Courtesy of Library of Congress
16-17	Associated Press
18	Courtesy of Library of Congress, Music Division
20	Associated Press
23	Used under license from iStockphoto.com
24	Associated Press
27	Associated Press
28	Photofest
30-31	Courtesy of Alsandro
33	Associated Press
38	Lebrecht Music and Arts Photo Library / Alamy
40	Courtesy of Library of Congress
43	Associated Press
45	Moviestore collection Ltd / Alamy
48	Bettmann/Corbis
51	Associated Press
53	Associated Press
55	Used under license from iStockphoto.com
57	Photo by BACHRACH
58	Heinz H. Weissenstein - Whitestone Photo – All Rights Reserved
61	Associated Press
64	Photofest
65	The New York Public Library for the Performing Arts/Billy Rose Theatre Division
67	Used under license from iStockphoto.com
68	Associated Press
71	Associated Press
73	Associated Press
74	INTERFOTO / Alamy
78	Associated Press
81	Used under license from iStockphoto.com
84	Associated Press
88	Courtesy of Library of Congress
90	Associated Press
94	Associated Press
95	Associated Press
97	Associated Press
100	DPA/Landov
105	Photo by Walter Scott/Courtesy of Boston Symphony Orchestra Archives

FEB 21 2014

HEWLETT-WOODMERE PUBLIC LIBRARY

3 1327 00582 4776

28 DAY LOAN

Hewlett-Woodmere Public Library
Hewlett, New York 11557-0903

Business Phone 516-374-1967
Recorded Announcements 516-374-1667